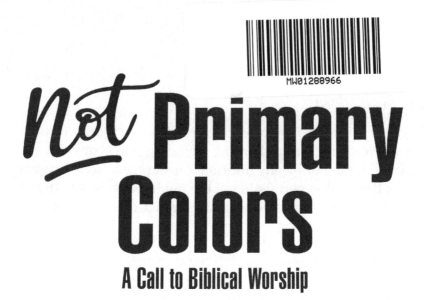

Not Primary Colors

A Call to Biblical Worship

Jon Hager, MD

NOT PRIMARY COLORS
by Jon Hager © 2019
All rights reserved

ISBN: 9781692128937

Book and cover design by Exodus Design Studio

Printed in the United States of America

Dedicated to:

My wife who has shown me what service is;

My mother who has shown me what surrender is;

My daughter who has shown me what sweetness is.

Contents

Prelude

Sing to the LORD a new song!
Sing to the LORD, all the earth!
Sing to the LORD! Praise his name!
Announce every day how he delivers!
Tell the nations about his splendor!
Tell all the nations about his amazing deeds!
For the LORD is great and certainly worthy of praise;
he is more awesome than all gods.
For all the gods of the nations are worthless,
but the LORD made the sky.
Majestic splendor emanates from him;
his sanctuary is firmly established and beautiful.
Ascribe to the LORD, O families of the nations,
ascribe to the LORD splendor and strength!
Ascribe to the LORD the splendor he deserves!
Bring an offering and enter his courts!
Worship the LORD in holy attire!
Tremble before him, all the earth!
Say among the nations, "The LORD reigns!
The world is established, it cannot be moved.
He judges the nations fairly."
Let the sky rejoice, and the earth be happy!
Let the sea and everything in it shout!
Let the fields and everything in them celebrate!
Then let the trees of the forest shout with joy
before the LORD, for he comes!
For he comes to judge the earth!
He judges the world fairly,
and the nations in accordance with his justice.
(*Psalm 96*)

Introduction
A Journey to Find Worship

"There. That adds some color and cheer," she remarked as she finished hanging the bright curtains. I nodded as I looked around at the otherwise bleak apartment that I'd been living in for over one year. The apartment was generously nicknamed the Shack by those who'd been there, and it was my attempt at saving money to pay off student loans while I was in ophthalmology residency. It was mostly below ground-level, and it had stark white walls and scanty brown carpet that dated it to the eighties. The fixtures and doors were mostly plastic and painted particle board, and there was a musty smell about the place that I was never able to eradicate.

Katherine, my wife-to-be and enthusiast of all things cheerful, loathed the place. Her charitable act of hanging the colorful curtains was something only a fiancée would care to do for a survivalist bachelor of thirty-one years.

I surveyed the apartment's new look. The curtains did add a nice touch of vibrancy to the pallid environment. It even made the view through the window of eye-level dirty snow and grey skies more tolerable.

My mind drifted to how my life could use an extra touch of color. I wished it could be as easy as hanging some curtains. My days in residency consisted of getting bludgeoned by austere supervisors, frequent shifts of call that could last forty hours, and difficult patients. I had little spiritual or social support. My apartment and the operating rooms I worked in were symbolic of my life—bleak and sterilized.

Throughout that difficult time, I turned to my walk with the Lord for joy and peace. But even my time with the Lord seemed monochromatic. Reading the Scriptures seemed familiar and routine—not in the good way. My prayers seemed to evaporate into the air as quickly as the vapor of my breath on those cold Iowa days. The smiles I presented to those in my church were contrived. Although my church family wanted to help me through this time, they could not. I felt completely alone, as though both people and God had forgotten about me. I longed to be able to taste and see some of God's goodness and abundant life.

My grayscale life needed color. I needed spiritual cataract surgery so I could see God not in faded tones, but in His true scintillating colors.

Slowly the Lord began to show me the vibrancy that worship and thanksgiving can bring to a washed-out life. I became convicted that in crying out to God for help, I was focused only on myself and my depression. No wonder my life was bleak, since I was focused more on my bleak circumstances than the magnificence of our God and Father. With subconscious arrogance, I was evaluating the King of the universe based on how much good He brought to my life. I was far from God because He felt far from me. I failed to worship Him for His goodness and faithfulness to me. My flesh told me, "If He ever shows you His goodness, *then* you can worship Him."

In His goodness, the Spirit fought against my flesh and showed me that I should be giving God thanks and worship as a daily part of my walk with Him. Worship is, after all, our original purpose and our eternal vocation. Thanksgiving is God's will for us (1 Thessalonians 5:18). The two are similar, yet sometimes different, as we'll discuss later.

As I embarked on the journey to implement more worship and thanksgiving in my life, I realized that thanksgiving came more naturally for me than worship. While I could offer extensive thanks to God, my prayers of worship felt contrived and were frequently derailed. In my interaction with others, I was comfortable showing gratitude to them or to God, but I felt conspicuous glorifying God to them.

When I did offer worship, I felt like an artist who painted only in primary colors: God is love, God is holy, God is just. Isn't there more to God's character than just those three things?

This led me on a journey to learn worship in my daily life. What is true worship? Why should I learn to worship? Isn't twenty minutes of worship on Sunday mornings enough? How can I use my spiritual eyes to see all of God's light and colors in worship, rather than settling for routine worship?

The Worshipful Heart

The worshipful heart is what God desires from us. To offer worship that's pleasing to Him, we don't need to be talented musicians, singers, or poets. We don't need to know the latest trendy praise songs or the heaviest hymns. God wants our hearts.

Growing up, my siblings and I gave my dad a mix of store-bought cards and handwritten cards for special occasions. The prefabricated cards were appreciated and loved, but our homemade cards (with "I love you" illegibly scribbled in crayon) were frequently and proudly hung on the walls in his office. I imagine that the same is true with God. If our hearts are in it, He undoubtedly loves when His children sing in unison to Him on Sunday mornings with prefabricated songs. But I imagine He takes special pleasure in the personal, heartfelt exaltation emanating from a life enriched by our knowing and loving Him.

It's not as much during corporate worship that God captures our imagination and fuels our desire for Him as it is in the sweet intimacy of our daily time alone with Him. As we passionately pursue individual worship of Him, He'll bring us into an even more intimate relationship with Him, while He whispers to our spirits new insights into His colorful nature.

However, worship should never be confined to the heart. Some in the church hide behind the "heart of worship" as an excuse to not vocalize our worship of God. We may say, "I live in a worshipful attitude," or, "I don't need to express my worship to truly be worshiping in my heart." This deprives us of an incredible blessing and experience that God gives us when we come before Him in His throne room. He wants each of us to individually worship Him in prayer and with others in conversational psalms, hymns, and spiritual songs (Ephesians 5:19). If we truly have a heart of worship, we'll express that worship in our prayers and conversations.

A Prelude to Worship

Such God-pleasing worship has two prerequisites.

First, we must make sure we sincerely desire to worship exclusively the God of the Bible as He reveals Himself to us. This of course is a constant battle and lifelong journey. We all worship something or someone—self, power, prestige, money, leisure, comfort, nature, chance, science, art, humanity, a hero, or whatever. Those of us who desire close fellowship with God rarely worship these worldly entities primarily, but often worship them alongside God. This is dangerous, but it has been happening since the beginning of time. Adam and Eve desired fellowship with God and self-promotion. The Israelites worshiped Yahweh and Baal. Samson worshiped God and his flesh. Hezekiah worshiped God as well as prestige and legacy.

Worshiping anything alongside God is idolatry. So we must ask ourselves: Do I worship God so I can win more favor with Him (self-advancement)? Do I worship Him so I can get blessings from Him (materialism)? Do I worship Him to appear more holy to others (spiritual status)? If this is the case, I urge you to open yourself up to the Lord, confess this idol worship to Him, and ask Him to change your heart to be thrilled with only Him and nothing else.

The second prerequisite to worship is living all of life in a way that's pleasing to God and in fellowship with Him. Otherwise, we can't offer authentic sacrifices of worship, for two reasons:

1. We cannot know God intimately if we're out of fellowship with Him. True worship is created in us as a response to the illumination of God's nature in our hearts by the Holy Spirit (1 Corinthians 2:12-13), who can be grieved by our sin against Him or by our insensitivity to Him. When we're out of fellowship with God, what we predominantly hear ringing in our ears are the voices of our flesh, the evil one, and the world. These voices tell us only lies about God and His relationship to us. True knowledge of God is essential for intimacy and worship.

2. God is pleased more by our obedience than our sacrifices (Hosea 6:6). There are no techniques, postures, or styles of songs that can make our worship pleasing to God if we're disobedient and out of fellowship with Him.

In 1 Samuel 15, King Saul tried to circumvent these prerequisites when he conquered the Amalekites while saving many of the animals God had told him to destroy. His stated reason for this (although I question his truthfulness) was so that he could sacrifice these choice animals to God. Because of Saul's self-willed disobedience, he was out of fellowship with God. Here is God's reply to him:

Does the LORD take pleasure in burnt offerings and sacrifices as much as he does in obedience? Certainly, obedience is better than sacrifice; paying attention is better than the fat of rams. (1 Samuel 15:22)

Keep yourself from idolatry, and maintain close fellowship with God if you want to cultivate worship in your life. Don't ignore prerequisites.

In a professional scenario, think of this: If you've never gone to law school, it's quite unlikely that you'll feel like a good lawyer, and less likely that you'll be a good lawyer, and no chance that you'll be qualified as a lawyer. Law school is a prerequisite to being a good lawyer. Trying to worship without the prerequisites is similar. If you feel that your worship life is lacking individually or corporately, you must ensure that you're progressing in fellowship with God and obedience to Him.

God describes Himself in Ezekiel 1 and Revelation 4 as having dazzling lights and the full spectrum of colors emanating from Him. Such description tells us that His nature is infinitely intense, complex and vibrant. We should worship Him in this way.

My prayer is that as you read this book, you develop a pervasive attitude of worship that is a sweet savor to God. I pray...

> that your worship adds vibrancy and depth to your walk with our Lord.

> that you see the beauty of creation and exclaim to those nearby, "The heavens declare the glory of God!"

> that you'll inquire of other believers how God showed Himself strong in the activities of their day.

> that you'll acknowledge God's sovereignty in every situation as you pray for the needs of others.

> that your worship life during the week makes you hungry for corporate worship and teaching on Sunday morning.

> that your life of worship becomes the flower of beauty in the desert of Christian self-preoccupation.

> that your worship makes your relationship with Christ winsome to those not having such a relationship.

> that your everyday view of God's splendor and majesty soars to the limits of your understanding, and that you dig deeper in Scripture to expand that limit.

It's my goal to help you worship even as you read this book. Worship should never be a mental or theoretical curiosity. To that end I'm including short scriptures, prayers, or hymns to assist you, under the repeated heading "*Selah.*" Please don't skip or skim over these; pause to worship with them, preferably at the end of your reading session.

As we change and our hearts become more devoted to worship, let's pray that we become a nation that boasts about the greatness of our God. May His name be magnified throughout our world. May we join together in one voice to express our awe and reverence of our Father and King not only on Sunday, but throughout our days. May those around us be drawn to their Creator by the expressed wonder that grips our hearts in His presence.

Chapter 1
Un-redefining Worship

Redefining a term can be a career-defining achievement. In academia, if you can convince your colleagues of the legitimacy of your new definition through a lengthy thesis, then you are sure to be published as an expert in the field. Redefinition can also result from an unintentional slippage of original use, usually caused by a slow cultural shift. For instance, "medical services" used to entail being seen by a physician who would take care of you no matter what your illness was or when it occurred, sometimes even going to your house to serve you. Because of cultural shift, "medical services" now involves being placed on hold when you call, fees for not showing to your appointment, physicians who are too busy to answer questions, exorbitant bills, and availability only 8:00-5:00 Monday through Thursday. The term has come to mean anything but service.

The concept of worship has suffered from redefinition, both intentional and unintentional. Ask the Christian next to you what they think of when worship is mentioned. Almost always, the answer will center on that period of the church service (from eight to forty-five minutes, depending on denomination) when the organ or guitar plays and someone in a suit or trendy street clothes stands in front of the congregation and leads them in singing. In the Bible which is our guidebook to worship, most of the worship is individual—prayers of humble exaltation or adoration stemming from intimacy with God or a brush with His magnificent glory. In these days, however, most books written about worship center on musical corporate worship and are devoted to topics such as how to lead others into deeper congregational worship and how to captivate the audience on Sunday mornings. These topics are worth exploring in detail. However, it's vital that Christians don't equate worship solely with a Sunday morning musical event. Hymns are not worship. Praise songs are not worship. Both can express worship, but they're nothing more than vehicles.

In *Worship by the Book*, D. A. Carson said the following:

> You cannot find excellent corporate worship until you stop trying to find excellent corporate worship and pursue God himself. Despite the protestations, one sometimes wonders if we are beginning to worship worship rather than worship God. As a brother put it to me, it's a bit like those who begin by admiring the sunset and soon begin to admire themselves admiring the sunset.

Carson is saying we're completely missing the point of worship because we've redefined it as something it isn't. By focusing on the music and band rather than the Lover of our souls, we've become aimless in our worship. We still call this "worship," but it's cheap and carries little of the goodness that true worship brings. The very thing that should satisfy our hearts with God's glory is starving us for it.

Redefining worship and relegating it to a fifteen-minute segment on Sunday mornings reminds me of the way my daughter sometimes used to take her bottle. She would hit her bottle on the ground, chew on the hard plastic part, and slobber all over it rather than actually sucking out the liquid. This frequently led to frustration, because merely chewing on hard plastic did not yield the expected result of nourishment. Technically, she was "taking the bottle," but got none of the taste or nutrients out of it. In worship, we can't expect to mindlessly follow a band for a few songs on Sunday morning and truly satisfy our spiritual need for worship. We must regain our aim by un-redefining worship and worshiping God irrespective of music, worship leaders, and performance.

The dictionary offers a definition of worship as "extravagant respect or admiration for or devotion to an object of esteem." This is a good generic definition of worship as it might relate to lovers or heroes; "he worships the ground she walks on." Noah Webster's 1828 dictionary is more profound in relation to our worship of God. It defines the act of worship as "to honor with extravagant love and extreme submission." This is a superior description of what our worship of God should look like because it adds the important aspect of submission. Submission ensures that we worship God for who He says He is and not who we want Him to be. It aides our understanding of God's attributes that are uncomfortable for us or that we don't like. And it guarantees that we won't come casually before God's throne, or with ulterior motives. Any problem with submission to God is a problem with worship.

Reorientation

So how does the Bible define worship? *Strong's Concordance* defines *proskyneo*—the Greek word most commonly used for worship in the New Testament—as "to kiss the ground while prostrating before a superior." The idea is that of total acknowledgment—in our spirit, body, mind, and will—of God's supremacy and our unworthiness. Similarly, in the Old Testament, the Hebrew word *shachaw* means to bow down, prostrate oneself, lie down. Once again, it's a demonstration of our true orientation to God. *Shachaw* is used in the following verses from the Psalms, where the bowing down of worship is paired with the metaphor of God's footstool, a place of humility relative to God's glory:

> *Praise* the LORD our God! Worship before his footstool! He is holy! (Psalm 99:5)

> *Let us go* to his dwelling place! Let us worship before his footstool! (Psalm 132:7)

From these two words—Greek *proskyneo* and Hebrew *shachaw*— we see that biblical worship is the submissive confession of the body, heart, and mind that supremely exalts God. It's not a series of compliments telling God and others that we approve of Him. His exalted nature is independent of our affirmation or even recognition.

When we examine the Scriptures to learn about who God is and who we intrinsically are, we realize that God's attributes aren't merely a better form of our attributes. In fact, many of His attributes are completely absent in us, such as His eternality, immutability, and transcendence. Others, such as His wisdom, kindness, and justice, are attributes we can display, but only imperfectly in comparison to God. He's the standard of the purest forms of all His attributes. All our attributes are tainted by sin, so we must say that God's attributes are completely other than ours—or rather, that our attributes are completely other than God's.

For instance, we cannot know exactly what God's love is because our love is tainted by selfishness. We can't perceive what absolute joy is because sin and sorrow have spoiled its purity and caused it to be relative. Because of God's revealed Word to us and the fact that we're created in His image, we can understand types of God's attributes, but we can never understand them fully. In Isaiah 55:9, God states, "For just as the sky is higher than the earth, so my deeds are superior to your deeds and my plans superior to your plans." This is infinite superiority—or really, supremacy.

As we grow in the realization of this disparity between ourselves and God, our view of God becomes higher, and we fall at His feet to worship Him in His perfection. The knowledge of His unknowability leaves us only to worship Him for His supremacy rather than to congratulate Him for relative superiority.

Worship thus flows from a rightfully high view of God in relationship to ourselves. The prophet Habakkuk understood how lofty God's attributes were when he asks questions about God's justice. Habakkuk's name means "ardent embrace," denoting either the grappling hold of a wrestler or a strong hug. Either way, it foretells the subject of his book in the Bible—first wrestling with God's supremacy, then embracing Him in worship. Habakkuk starts out on what seems like shaky ground as he questions God:

> *Why do you force me to witness injustice? Why do you put up with wrongdoing? Destruction and violence confront me; conflict is present and one must endure strife. For this reason the law lacks power, and justice is never carried out. Indeed, the wicked intimidate the innocent. For this reason justice is perverted.* (Habakkuk 1:3-4)

The Lord is kind and gentle in His reply in 1:5-11. He states that He's about to raise the Babylonians in power for His purposes. Habakkuk, still bewildered, responds by confessing God's sovereignty as he wrestles with understanding how God's plans conform to His attributes:

> *LORD, you have been active from ancient times; my sovereign God, you are immortal. LORD, you have made them your instrument of judgment. Protector, you have appointed them as your instrument of punishment. You are too just to tolerate evil; you are unable to condone wrongdoing. So why do you put up with such treacherous people? Why do you say nothing when the wicked devour those more righteous than they are?* (1:12-13)

Habakkuk worshipfully starts with known truth about God's attributes. God is active in our affairs. He is sovereign. He is immortal. He's our protector. He is just. But there are issues Habakkuk doesn't completely understand, and they seem to contradict his knowledge of God. The Lord is Israel's protector, yet He's using the Babylonians as instruments of judgment. He is just, yet it seems He's tolerating evil and condoning wrongdoing.

Rather than doubting God's attributes because of this apparent dissonance, Habakkuk remembers his rightful place beneath God's footstool. He doesn't assert his knowledge or perspective, but rather does something remarkable in 2:1. He listens. He asks to be taught of the Lord concerning God's nature and plans. His heart yearns to learn of God and to gain a higher view of Him. He isn't imagining himself to be in the center of the universe, demanding that the Lord fit into his human perceptions of Him or how things should be. He's begging the Lord to instruct him and give him a higher and more theocentric viewpoint.

After the Lord does this, Habakkuk breaks out into a beautiful and worshipful prayer in chapter 3. Here are a few excerpts:

> *Lord, I have heard the report of what you did; I am awed, LORD, by what you accomplished.* (3:2)
>
> *He takes his battle position and shakes the earth; with a mere look He frightens the nations.*
>
> *The ancient mountains disintegrate; the primeval hills are flattened. He travels on the ancient roads.* (3:6)
>
> *When the fig tree does not bud, and there are no grapes on the vines; when the olive trees do not produce, and the fields yield no crops; when the sheep disappear from the pen, and there are no cattle in the stalls, I will rejoice because of the LORD; I will be happy because of the God who delivers me!*
>
> *The sovereign LORD is my source of strength.*
>
> *He gives me the agility of a deer; He enables me to negotiate the rugged terrain.* (3:17-19)

Habakkuk's high view of God produces worship without complete comprehension of God's plan and His attributes. He's able to rejoice in the Lord even when facing hardship and difficulty, when God doesn't seem good to him. This is the result of seeing God in the center stage of the universe and reorienting ourselves to our rightful positions. Before salvation, we were merely spectators of God's great plan. Now we're saved by God's grace to be included in His cosmic plan, graciously allowed to take a small supporting role as He builds His kingdom.

We must ask ourselves: What if this entire life is all about God's glory and not primarily my own perceived well-being? What if the whole universe exists to bring God glory, and every event is ordained for that purpose? It is. Our circumstances don't affect the building of God's kingdom. The building of God's kingdom affects our circumstances.

Not only does reorientation lead to worship, but worship leads to reorientation. And oh, how often we need that reorientation! Life's problems—all of them—can be completely solved only by worshipfully bowing to God as the reason for our existence. The universe is His stage, and worship helps us realize this perspective.

When I was a youth pastor, I decided one day to take some of my youths on an all-day river-tubing trip from one city to another. I didn't check the map, feeling confident I knew the area well enough. If asked, I would have estimated the distance to be several miles, which would take us between four and eight hours. We got a late start, leaving at noon, but I had my cell phone in a plastic bag in case we took longer than expected, so what could go wrong?

As the sun was setting after we'd spent eight hours on the river, I realized that my cell phone had gotten wet, and we seemed nowhere close to our destination. I had no clue where we were. Sometime after midnight, we bailed out and got off the river, traipsing through snake-infested, cactus-laden hill country wilderness. After about four hours of hiking, we finally found our way back to a house around five a.m. Thankfully, I didn't find myself staring up the barrel of a gun the following Sunday at church, but there were a few slaps to the back of my head.

If only we'd been able to view our situation from on high, we would have been able to reorient ourselves. We would have realized that the river's course was much longer than what we thought it was from our perspective. We would have left the river sooner, and found the solution to our problem. The same is true in our spiritual lives. Worship gives us the essential high perspective that tells our hearts how much bigger God's plan is than primarily our struggles and joys.

The book of Psalms gives many examples of worship leading to the reorientation of our hearts. It includes many prayers that start with a depressed or self-focused tone. Usually, by the middle of the psalm, that tone gives way to pivotal worship and rejoicing. These psalms frequently end with joyful celebration of a relationship with God.

Psalm 71 is a good example. In verses 1-13, the psalmist pleads for God's help and mercy against his wicked and unrighteous enemies. The next verses are pivotal:

> *As for me, I will wait continually, and will continue to praise you. I will tell about your justice, and all day long proclaim your salvation, though I cannot fathom its full extent. I will come and tell about the mighty acts of the sovereign LORD. I will proclaim your justice—yours alone.* (71:14-16)

This transition of worship lifts his soul from its despair and places his focus on God's greatness rather than on his perceived poor circumstances. Focusing on our lowliness without seeing God's greatness leads only to depression and anxiety.

The psalm ends in joyful confidence:

> *My lips will shout for joy! Yes, I will sing your praises! I will praise you when you rescue me! All day long my tongue will also tell about your justice, for those who want to harm me will be embarrassed and ashamed.* (71:23-24)

When we worship Him, our thinking and our focus change so that He's in His rightful place on the throne—rather than our problems and sorrows being there.

Selah

Who has measured out the waters in the hollow of his hand, or carefully measured the sky, or carefully weighed the soil of the earth, or weighed the mountains in a balance, or the hills on scales?

Who comprehends the mind of the LORD, or gives him instruction as his counselor?

From whom does he receive directions?

Who teaches him the correct way to do things, or imparts knowledge to him, or instructs him in skillful design?

Look, the nations are like a drop in a bucket; they are regarded as dust on the scales.

He lifts the coastlands as if they were dust.
(Isaiah 40:12-15)

We are a moment, You are forever,
Lord of the ages, God before time;
We are a vapor, You are eternal,
Love everlasting, reigning on high.
Holy, Holy, Lord God Almighty,
Worthy is the Lamb who was slain;
Highest praises, honor, and glory
Be unto Your name, Be unto Your name
(Lynn Deshazo and Gary Sadler)

From the Ground

The key to worshipful reorientation is submission and humility. When we go back to the origin of the word *proskyneo*, we see that the essence of the word includes a deliberate acknowledgment of our humble state. This was demonstrated beautifully by the wise men in

Matthew 2, as they come to visit the young child Jesus. Imagine these extremely rich, prominent, and knowledgeable men entering the humble abode of this family to meet the young child. They show no signs of expecting a ceremonious greeting worthy of their status. More impressively, they didn't treat Jesus as a respected equal: "After coming into the house they saw the Child with Mary His mother; and they fell to the ground and worshiped Him" (Matthew 2:11 NASB).

In the New Testament's original Greek language, two words are used together to describe the wise men's actions before Jesus: *pesontes* ("having fallen down") and *proskyneo* ("they worshiped"). Applying what we've learned about *proskyneo*, this phrase is saying, "Having fallen down, they kissed the ground." These men of high status and prominence didn't think twice about being on the ground in a humble house before a young child. Their humility was obviously both external and internal. Not for show, but genuine. Not subdued, but complete. We should never shy away from this type of humility before our God and King.

Instead of falling to the ground and worshiping before the Lord's supremacy in genuine and complete humility, we often esteem our own reasoning as being equal to God's wisdom, although we might never say as much. We have our parts of Scripture that we love and preach, and other parts that we avoid. Sometimes we use Scripture as a weapon against others in argument, rather than submitting our way of living to it. Sometimes we even massage the Scriptures to communicate a popular message that will appeal to the hearers, even when we violate the true meaning of the Word. What a crime against God and humanity to use our own reasoning to manipulate God's message to other people!

Years ago, I heard a pastor speak after Hurricane Katrina ravaged Louisiana. He posed a question: "Why do bad things like this happen to good people?" I thought this oft-asked question was particularly relevant and looked forward to hearing a scriptural answer. Unfortunately, my interest turned to disgust as he posed a false dilemma with three postulates: Either 1) God is all-loving, or 2) God is all-powerful, or 3) bad things don't happen to good people. To my astonishment and horror, he concluded that God is all-loving but not all-powerful.

Such a cosmic-scale judgment shows extreme pride and arrogance. By contradicting doctrines of God's attributes because he couldn't fully comprehend them, this man lofted his own wisdom above God's. A humble and submissive heart (such as Habakkuk's) would acknowledge God's greatness and all His attributes even though we don't fully understand them. This isn't to say we aren't allowed to question the nature of circumstances we perceive to be bad. But we should question them from our rightful position—of being prostrate at the foot of God's throne, in our spirit at least.

Maybe we don't err so blatantly as to contradict God's attributes from a pulpit. Maybe we rather question in our hearts whether what God says in His Word is true when we're so beat up that we can't sense God's love or power in our lives. Or we might become bitter and vengeful because it doesn't seem like God hasn't noticed the wrong done to us by an evil person. But we're too small to fully see how His hand works for the glory of His kingdom, so we must worship Him in faith and humility. Our feelings about Him don't trump the truth of His Word, and we must subordinate them to His truth in worship.

Job fell into iniquity when he questioned God using "words without knowledge." He mistakenly assumed that he, rather than God's great plan, was at the center of the universe. He didn't understand that greater things were going on which he didn't know about, so he boldly questioned God in the middle portion of the book. He might have averted God's reproof had he stayed spiritually prostrate, as he seemed to be in the beginning when he said,

Naked I came from my mother's womb, and naked I will return there. The LORD gives, and the LORD takes away. May the name of the LORD be blessed. (Job 1:21)

Let's always remember our proper state of humility as we reorient ourselves to the ground and ascribe greatness to God. This doesn't necessarily mean we beat ourselves and focus on how wretched we are. That in itself can be a form of self-worship and adoration. Instead, we see ourselves as God sees us—without any ability to achieve worth on our own, but worthy beyond price because of Christ's righteousness imputed to us, and His inexplicable delight in us.

When we fail in reorientation and in humility before God's throne, worship becomes unimportant to us. We become casual and neglectful of the very thing for which we were created. Of course, this failure isn't necessarily a hatred of God, since we all fail to worship God as we should. The failure shows up in most of our lives as an oversight created by egocentrism.

Egocentrism: Antonym of Biblical Worship

At its heart, worship is acknowledging that God is on the throne, and all things are subordinate to Him in every way. Egocentrism is elevating my desires and needs to the throne and subordinating God and others to them. Worship and egocentrism are diametrically opposed to each other, engaging in a battle for control over our souls. It's the cosmic battle that took place between Christ and Satan in the wilderness two millennia ago, when Satan appealed to Christ's needs and desires. Unfortunately, egocentrism dominates our culture, both in society and in the church. It is insidious in how it places the individual's needs and desires—even good ones—on the throne of one's life.

Sometimes egocentrism even shows up as redefined worship (though it's actually the opposite of biblical worship). In this scenario, we "worship" in the way that makes us feel happy, and for the things that make us feel happy, and only when it's convenient for us. As long as we're happy and satisfied, then God is sovereign and worthy of worship. This mindset derails us from true worship.

Because of our egocentrism, we've become consumed with pursuits of ease, leisure, self-advancement, comfort, prestige, popularity, and power. Because of this, our flesh, the world's system, and the evil one are all busy ensuring that we have a high view of our personal needs and desires. So we bedazzle ourselves with trinkets, ignoring our chief purpose on earth of worshiping God and of making other rebels like ourselves into worshipers of God. We let rot God's offer to us of His spiritual riches and glory here and now, taking for granted that they'll be waiting for us in heaven. This has caused us to become impotent as a church. We should, in contrast, worship intentionally by placing God on the throne above all, and by being thrilled with the knowledge and praise of Him.

God's transcendence of course doesn't depend on our acknowledgment of it, but we enrich our own lives when we worship. It helps us reorient ourselves to our proper relationship with God — with Him at the center of all things, and us in awe of His splendor, power, and love. Just as thanksgiving is the antidote to complaining, true worship is the antidote to egocentrism.

When this contrast is drawn between worship and the depravity of egocentrism, it's probably not difficult for you to realize theoretically the superior value of worship. Moreover, it would seem that we should easily and instinctively desire to worship God since we spend our time in God's universe that declares His glory, and in His house where His people meet, and in His throne room where He meets with each of us individually during our prayer time with Him. So it shouldn't be too difficult to find displays of worship in everyday encounters with Christians. Unfortunately, this is often not the case, and we see egocentrism more commonly than worship. We see couples losing opportunities for spiritual and emotional intimacy with each other because they would rather be on their cell phones than conversing with each other about the goodness of the Lord. We check sports scores during church sermons because we're bored by listening to the teaching of the Word of God (ironically, right after the "worship segment").

Egocentrism doesn't necessarily equate to active and deliberate rebellion or hatred of God. However, it does fuel most of our reasons for not being worship-centered people. Are you too busy to worship? That's egocentrism. Are you self-conscious about vocalized worship? That's egocentrism. Is our view of God unintentionally too low because we haven't put forth effort to learn of Him? Egocentrism. If we're committed to living a life that's pleasing to God and full of joy and meaning, we must put aside our egocentrism in order to worship.

Study Questions

1. How do you currently implement worship in your walk with God? How would you like to?

2. What are some ways that egocentrism shows up in your life? What are some ways to overcome this?

3. Read Ezekiel 43:6-7. The temple was called God's footstool and was the place of worship and sacrifice for the Israelites. How do we worship from God's footstool in today's age?

Chapter 2
Characteristics of Worship

What is a tomato? That's easy. It's a round vegetable from the plant *Solanum lycopersicum*, right? Technically, that's a correct definition, but if you want to develop your knowledge of what a tomato really is, you must go beyond definitions to characteristics. Tomatoes can be red, yellow, orange, purple, green, or striped. They're high in sugar, vitamin C, fiber, water, and lycopene. They can be cooked, dried, or eaten raw. Homegrown are always better than store-bought. Although the definition of a tomato is an important starting point, one can spend a lifetime learning the characteristics of tomatoes beyond the basic definition.

Remember our definition of worship from Noah Webster's 1828 dictionary: "to honor with extravagant love and extreme submission." This is a great starting definition for the worship of our God, but there are additional characteristics that are essential to understanding and offering worship. Let's explore God's multifaceted revelation of worship in His Word one characteristic at a time. The beauty of worshiping our great God is that when these characteristics are present, a simple child can offer worship as pleasing to God as the most brilliant theologian. There's danger however, in mindlessly assuming that our past habits of worship are true worship. Just as sincere intentions cannot save us from our sin, our knowledge or passion doesn't necessarily equal worship. So before we look at the characteristics of true worship, let's clarify what worship is not.

Beyond the Music

The essence of worship is much more than music and singing.

When I was in college, I ventured out one night to a Christian ministry's meeting. It was held under the floor of the basketball arena. As I traversed the tunnels, not knowing exactly where I was going, I began to hear music with vulgar lyrics. Although I surmised that this wouldn't be the ministry, I expected that the owners of this music might know where the ministry was located. I headed toward the music. When I entered the room, it was full of college students partying and dancing to the music (quite suggestively in some cases). Confused, I asked if this was the Christian meeting and was assured that it was. I surveyed the room in disbelief. Women were clad in revealing clothing, leaving little of their fleshly desires to the imagination. Men were jumping around performing the raunchy lyrics along with the music, known to them by heart.

Suddenly the music stopped. There was a short call to "worship" and the house band started playing. Immediately, the people in the room assumed the "worship position": swaying gently back and forth, eyes closed, and both hands in the air. Some even sank to their knees, covering their eyes as if they were suddenly "broken" after their display of hip thrusts and gyrations only two minutes earlier. I found myself judging them for their false worship, completely distracted from the blessed opportunity to give our Lord praise. Later, I confessed my judgmental attitude to the Lord, realizing that my distracted "worship" was no more authentic than that of those around me.

Worship transcends music and singing. If we live as we please, then hurdle haphazardly into a twenty-minute worship "experience," longing for a warm and tingly feeling, this is not worship. If we mouth the words of worship songs while thinking sinful, judgmental, or distracted thoughts, this is not worship.

At Baylor College of Medicine in 2007, I sat in class listening to a tidal wave of information, feverishly taking notes. The topic on this particular day was a summary of cell physiology describing how all the pieces fit together. The lecturer eloquently related each organelle and its function to each other to describe the intricacy of the cell. As I became enraptured by the flawless design of these microscopic cells which put our machines and computers to shame, my note-taking lagged. The thrill and wonder of God's omnipotence and omniscience seized me, and I worshiped in my heart and mind. The lecturer continued the rushed dissertation, but the Spirit of Him who created me, loved me, and gave Himself for me had my full attention, and I couldn't help but praise Him for His wonderful creation.

The first example took place in a "service of worship," with a band meant to lead into worship with songs that had worshipful words. But there, worship failed. In the second example, a terrified medical student was trying to keep his head above water, in the middle of a weekday, in the most secular of institutions. Yet the purest expression of worship broke forth.

This calls into question our modern Christian intellectual construct of worship. When we examine the Scriptures for examples of worship, we don't find descriptions of the emotional tension or crowds of people at one of David's electric harp concerts ("Put your hands together, Gath. I caaan't heeeaar yoooou"). There certainly are accounts of corporate worship, but the vast majority of worship in the Bible is individual.

So on to the characteristics of worship. Learning scriptural characteristics of worship is vital for your individual worship and walk with the Lord. When a church hires a new worship pastor, we would expect the interview to focus on the worship pastor's understanding of what the characteristics of biblical corporate worship are. However, in your quiet times with the Lord, you don't have a human pastor to lead you into worship. It's just you and the Holy Spirit (the ultimate worship leader) in the very presence of God.

Learn all the characteristics of worship. We tend to love one or two aspects of worship and ignore the others. That will lead us into a malnourished life of worship.

When I was in medical school and residency, I was an expert at finding nurses' stations that retained sheet-cakes from various celebrations. I had little time to cook and no money, so leftover sheet-cakes became a dietary staple I sometimes lived on for days at a time. They were free and easy, and I could technically survive on the calories they provided. Don't settle for sheet-cake worship that's convenient and will allow your malnourished spiritual life to technically survive. We want to live a balanced diet of spiritually nutritious worship.

Worship Is a Celebration

What a joy that we can worship such a perfect God! For those who've trusted Christ, there's no angst or uncertainty mixed into worshiping Him, as there is with worshiping anyone or anything else. Those who worship secular deities such as money, power, and fame must fear the loss of those things, and often spend their lives trying to ensure against it. Those who religiously worship false gods fear that their goodness may be inadequate, and they spend their lives performing rituals hoping to gain favor with God. But believers in Christ know that He has already bought infinite favor for us with God—meaning that we cannot add to or subtract from that favor by anything we do or say.

Because of this, worship is a pure celebration. J. I. Packer expressed it this way:

> We need to discover all over again that worship is natural to the Christian, as it was to the godly Israelites who wrote the Psalms, and that the habit of celebrating the greatness and graciousness of God yields an endless flow of thankfulness, joy, and zeal.

If we worship God to gain favor with Him, we're worshiping for our own advantage and falling into the trap of egocentrism—really worshiping our needs and desires. This is why "worship" in all the works-based religions are merely a form of self-worship and attempted self-preservation. God's grace, extended to us at the time of salvation, and based on Christ's imputation of His righteousness to us, allows us to truly worship God for His magnificence rather than for our spiritual credit accounts.

It's a reality that the prophet Isaiah foresaw and so beautifully expressed:

> *I will greatly rejoice in the* LORD; *I will be overjoyed because of my God. For he clothes me in garments of deliverance; he puts on me a robe symbolizing vindication. I look like a bridegroom when he wears a turban as a priest would; I look like a bride when she puts on her jewelry.* (Isaiah 61:10)

Hallelujah! What joy and celebration this should bring to us as we worship Him! As N. T. Wright says about worship,

> It is the glad shout of praise that arises to God the creator and God the rescuer from the creation that recognizes its maker, the creation that acknowledges the triumph of Jesus the Lamb. That is the worship that is going on in heaven, in God's dimension, all the time. The question we ought to be asking is how best we might join in.

There's great entertainment in watching people fall in love. We see sloppy boys square their shoulders and become men when they meet the woman of their dreams. We see homely and shy girls become beaming, radiant women. Common to nearly all of them is the incessant chatter of new love. If you've ever had a close friend fall in love, you've probably borne the brunt of such gushing. Wouldn't it suffice for her to say, "He's godly, smart, talented, beautiful, outgoing, and practically perfect in every way"? There, that takes five seconds. Instead, over a forty-five-minute conversation, you hear every detail about how this guy has the same dimple a famous actor has, how he likes his coffee the same way she does, and how he makes her feel so special when he says her name. One cannot help but smile at their exuberance and celebrate with them their newly found love.

We're the object of God's love, and if you want to hear gushing, read the Song of Solomon. God heartily approves of gushing within marriage—and, as an allegorical extension, in His relationship with His people. God is evidently overflowing with love and passion for His people. In response to His love, worship for us—like the bride's effusive words in the Song of Solomon—is a gushing celebration of our relationship with Him. When we know and love Him as we ought, it's a natural reaction for us to gush to others about His tender care for us, His control of all situations, His holiness which will allow us to spend eternity without the presence of sin, and an infinite number of other things about Him.

This worshipful celebration also makes our faith winsome to others. Incessantly bragging on God's greatness is likely to be more appealing to unbelieving friends than cornering them and asking where they would go if they died tonight. Some Christians mistakenly characterize the walk of faith as burdensome, with a list of do's and don'ts. Although it's gravely important to obey Christ's commands as our way of loving Him (as Jesus tells us in John 14:21), we can get bogged down as the Pharisees did if we focus only on our actions. Trying to avoid this, some Christians wrongly target Christ's commands as the source of legalism, and they err on the side of liberty in order to not be pharisaical. That's the wrong reaction. Instead, when worship and thanksgiving permeate every area of our lives, it will lead to overflowing joy and peace, which makes our witnessing so much easier. The rarity of a soul filled with joy and peace will make our faith attractive to others.

Of course, the true gospel absolutely must be shared in witnessing, but the celebration of worship can open the doors in conversation. Joy and peace are what everyone in this world is looking for — but in the wrong places if not in Christ. Others who see our lives bubbling over will want what we have. We cannot convince others of Christ's attractiveness if He's not attractive to us.

So don't read this book and add worship to a list of formulas required for the successful Christian life. Lose yourself in the celebration of His greatness. Sing and dance before Him and Him alone. He has redeemed your soul with His blood so that you can celebrate Him without fear, restraint, or hesitation.

Worship Is an Experience

A Christian author I greatly respect wrote that worship is not an experience but rather an act that takes discipline, irrespective of our feelings. While it's true that worship is an act and does take discipline, and that it might be irrespective of feelings, this doesn't encompass the totality of worship. Worship is the experience of entering the throne room of God and responding to His grandeur — as we see in this passage:

> *In the year of King Uzziah's death, I saw the Lord seated on a high, elevated throne. The hem of his robe filled the temple. Seraphs stood over him; each one had six wings. With two wings they covered their faces, with two they covered their feet, and they used the remaining two to fly. They called out to one another, "Holy, holy, holy is the LORD of heaven's armies! His majestic splendor fills the entire earth!" The sound of their voices shook the door frames, and the temple was filled with smoke.*
>
> *I said, "Woe is me! I am destroyed, for my lips are contaminated by sin, and I live among people whose lips are contaminated by sin. My eyes have seen the king, the LORD of heaven's armies." (Isaiah 6:1-5)*

Isaiah sees this vision of the great King of the universe clothed in

His majesty, with angelic beings crying out to one another while worshiping God in His holiness. These are not things one ordinarily sees. This experience drives Isaiah onto the ground "as a dead man," and causes him to see his own sin and God's majesty and holiness. What else is there for him to do but confess his lowliness and God's greatness?

When an individual experiences God, two things happen that we see from Scripture.

First, there's the *impression* of God's glory. The person typically falls down "as dead" from dismay over their own sinfulness and awe of God's glory. John does this in Revelation 1. Throughout the Scriptures, these encounters are usually experienced by believers who don't fear eternal separation from God. They know that Christ's righteousness has been imputed to them and that their sin has been forgiven, yet they still fall to the ground. If we truly wish to experience God in worship, we must be ready to be crushed in the agony of realizing the magnitude of our sin against a holy and righteous God, even if we know our sins are forgiven. Our churches need more experience of God, but it's not the sappy experience we sing about while hugging ourselves and becoming emotional over the music. It's the Revelation 1 type of experience that we need—the true experience of God that causes us to bow down in fear, awe, and worship. If God physically showed up in one of our corporate worship times, what a change that would bring!

Second, there's a *confession* of God's glory. "My eyes have seen the king, the LORD who commands armies," Isaiah exclaims. This confession is a reaction to the impression of God's glory. It isn't mouthing words set in front of us, or singing along with a tune that makes us feel good. If our confessions about God are borne from anything less than the knowledge and experience of the eternal God and His vast attributes, we're missing out on true worship.

It's easy to get stuck on the things that we "like" about God—things that make us feel happy, valued, or safe. When our focus stays there, we run the risk of painting our own picture of who we want

God to be. This is worship not of God, but of our idealized self, or of the idealized world over which we wish to be god.

Although worship *is* an experience—a true spiritual entering into the throne room of the King of the universe—we cannot allow our worship to be *led* by experiential feelings. We may feel something spectacular, or we may not. Certainly, not all worship will feel like a profound experience. This is true especially of our quick mentions to others of God's glory. Worship should not be dictated by the lack of those feelings, and we definitely shouldn't depend on visions or out-of-body experiences to come before God in worship. We can experience Him through His revealed nature in the Word. All we need for a true worship experience is the stirring of the Holy Spirit as we meditate on His Word.

It's no coincidence that in Revelation 1, immediately before his visions starts, John states that he "was in the Spirit on the Lord's day." When we don't experience God as we would like, it's often because we're not "in the Spirit." We must experience God in worship through the pages of Scripture and by the teaching of His Spirit rather than merely turning up the music or reading inspirational quotes, which may serve more as a distraction.

Although we sometimes try to separate knowledge, experience, and study from worship, we cannot. That's like trying to make chocolate chip cookies without flour or sugar. We must submerge ourselves in the Word under the guidance of the Holy Spirit in order to truly experience God in worship. Then the windows of our hearts will burst open, and we'll experience the vast glory of our King, the Lord of hosts in His throne room.

Worship Is an Attitude

Although worship is an experience of bowing before God in His throne room, we're misguided if we perceive worship as *all* experience. If we worship God only when we feel the experience of Him, our worship lives become shallow and dependent on extrinsic factors. Worship is an attitude that proceeds from a heart and mind steeped in God's Word.

Consider Paul's exulting words at the end of Romans 11. He has just discussed in detail the mysteries of salvation and how both Jews and Gentiles fit into God's plan for His family and kingdom. As he's writing and elucidating the mind of God, Paul can restrain himself no longer and bursts out:

> *Oh, the depth of the riches and wisdom and knowledge of God! How unsearchable are his judgments and how fathomless his ways! For who has known the mind of the Lord, or who has been his counselor? Or who has first given to God, that God needs to repay him? For from him and through him and to him are all things. To him be glory forever! Amen.* (Romans 11:33-36)

As Paul demonstrates, close fellowship and intimacy with God produce an attitude of being ever mindful of worship. It's from this attitude that true worship must be offered, or else it's contrived. This attitude isn't cultivated instantly every Sunday morning for twenty minutes. It must be fed during the week with high thoughts of God that come from His Word and from His Spirit. Otherwise, our warm and fuzzy feelings during "praise and worship" time are likely nothing more than the same emotional response to the music that anybody would feel at a concert. *Those who don't worship during the week are unlikely to truly worship Sunday mornings.*

John Piper spoke of this attitude of constant communion with God: "We belittle God when we go through the outward motions of worship and take no pleasure in His person."

George Washington was a devout Christian, and lived his life as an example of someone whose attitude of worship was strong in his personal relationship with God. This devotion overflowed from his heart into the communal time of worship and was observed in a church service by the Reverend Lee Massey, who wrote of Washington, "His behavior in the house of God was ever so deeply reverential that it produced the happiest effects on my congregation, and greatly assisted me in my pulpit labors." What a compliment! Massey's observation that a reverential attitude and behavior can influence an entire congregation should be a teaching point for each of us. Our behavior and attitude always impact those around us, and what better impact can we ask for than assisting God's laborers in their work?

This behavior and attitude cannot be appropriated on demand for Sunday mornings. If we look to George Washington's prayer life, we see reverence emanating from his personal walk with the Lord.

Here's part of a prayer he recorded at age twenty:

> Almighty and eternal Lord God, the great creator of heaven & earth, and the God and Father of our Lord Jesus Christ; look down from heaven, in pity and compassion upon me thy servant, who humbly prostrate myself before thee, sensible of thy mercy and my own misery; there is an infinite distance between thy glorious majesty and me, thy poor creature, the work of thy hand; between thy infinite power, and my weakness; thy wisdom, and my folly; thine eternal Being, and my mortal frame. But, O Lord, I have set myself at a greater distance from thee by my sin and wickedness, and humbly acknowledge the corruption of my nature and the many rebellions of my life.

Notice his high view of God, his realistic view of himself, his humility in declaring his failures, and his eagerness to declare God's greatness and his failures. Those who have this attitude of worship in their personal walk with the Lord will truly experience the Lord in every aspect of life, including Sunday morning corporate worship.

As mentioned previously, we shouldn't try to divorce this attitude of worship from our experience of worship. I've seen believers walk down the path of completely academic spirituality, and they often miss the mark of true sanctification. These are the people of whom it's said that they're too heavenly minded to be of any earthly good.

The reality, however, is that a heavenly minded believer will desire to experience God on earth as vividly as we'll experience Him in heaven. We'll want to taste and see that the Lord is good. Our emotions will worship Him alongside our spirits and intellect. Otherwise, we become spiritually mechanical, opening ourselves up to legalism and disenchantment.

An attitude of worship, when cultivated and combined with other characteristics of worship, will guarantee that God is glorified in everything we do, whether reading the Bible, studying doctrine, or serving others. It will also put to rest the argument of whether praise songs or hymns are better vehicles of worship. When our hearts long to worship God and are in a constant attitude of worship, the vehicle for that worship won't matter. Postures become unimportant. Our own vocal quality or that of the person in front of us at church becomes unnoticed, because it's only the grandeur of the Lord that matters to us. And from that attitude, worship is expressed.

Worship Is an Expression

Imagine a marriage in which the husband never tells his wife that she's beautiful to him, because "it goes without saying." What if the wife never expressed admiration for her husband, because "actions speak louder than words." Imagine a child who never heard the words "I love you," because the parents assume that feeding and clothing the child should be enough expression of love. (You may not have to imagine such things at all, remembering your own experiences of them.)

We are meant to be expressive beings. We're created in God's image, who glorifies and expresses His love for His Son, as we're reminded when the apostle Peter says the following about Jesus:

For he received honor and glory from God the Father, when that voice was conveyed to him by the Majestic Glory: "This is my dear Son, in whom I am delighted." (2 Peter 1:17)

Notice that God not only glorifies His Son, but also expresses here to human beings the pleasure that He takes in His Son. God makes similar expressions several other times in Scripture—most notably at Jesus's baptism and at His transfiguration. God didn't need to express His pleasure in Christ to validate Christ's message. At the transfiguration, He could have easily said, "This is my Son. Listen to Him." Instead He says, "This is my one dear Son, in whom I take great delight. Listen to Him." (Matthew 17:5).

Jesus speaks of this love in John 17, where He mentions three times (in verses 23, 24, and 26) the love the Father has for the Son. Rather than keeping Their love for each other completely intimate, the Son and the Father want all of us to know how much They love each other. Interestingly, Jesus connects the Father's love to the glory the Father gave the Son before the world's creation:

Father, I want those you have given me to be with me where I am, so that they can see my glory that you gave me because you loved me before the creation of the world. (17:24)

This is a beautiful example for us to follow—that our worship of God's glory, though far from perfect, is an expression of our love for Him.

One of the most beautiful expressions of worship in the Bible is that of the woman who washed Jesus's feet with her tears and perfume (Luke 7:36-50). This woman understood that because of her gesture, she could fall quickly into harsh criticism. She was, after all, a sinner going into the house of a respected religious leader. Ignoring all concern, she got on the ground, wet Jesus's feet with her tears, and kept kissing them (again and again) and wiping them with her hair. She knew God's exalted nature and her place of lowliness, and she expressed her worship. Although she could have been content with her experience of Jesus and her attitude of exaltation, she still humbled herself in an outward expression of personal and private worship.

The Lord was touched by such a rare expression, because this woman truly believed what we all say we believe: that we're unworthy sinners in desperate need of forgiveness before a holy God.

Earlier in this passage, Jesus did not give Simon the Pharisee "partial credit" for some sort of internal affinity toward God. Jesus remarked that Simon did not even give him water for washing or a kiss of greeting; Jesus disparaged him in comparison to the prostitute who'd expressed her worship. Conversely, Jesus acknowledged that the woman's expression of humility and exaltation of God showed a heart full of faith and repentance, resulting in the forgiveness of her sins.

We must not use personality type as an excuse for not outwardly expressing our worship of God. We who tend toward self-consciousness or introversion may try to hide behind our personalities, which we claim aren't conducive to expressive worship. However, based on God the Father's example of His expressed glorification of the Son, we should shun the notion that our love and worship of God can be solely intimate in nature, and doesn't need to be demonstrated.

Remember what Jesus said: "For whoever is ashamed of me and my words, the Son of Man will be ashamed of that person when he comes in his glory and in the glory of the Father and of the holy angels" (Luke 9:26). We should yearn above all else to someday hear God's unmuted expression to us, "Well done, good and faithful servant."

Of course, this doesn't mean we need to stand on the street corner with a megaphone, dance about in church with our arms raised, or pray with dramatic and impassioned tones (unless, of course, the

Lord leads you to these things). The worship of the Holy One has no formula. It may be that the deep study of Bible doctrine leads your heart to fall prostrate before God's throne, expressing worship in prayers or in deep theological conversation saturated with praise. Or your heart may celebrate with more visible expression when exposed to a touching song, beautiful sunset, or striking Bible verse. Worship in everyday prayer and conversation allows us to fulfill our purpose without the necessity of shouting "Amen!" in church, if that's not your style. However, if you excuse yourself from expressive worship in church because that's not your style, you have no choice but to immerse yourself in a lifestyle of expressive worship in prayer and conversation.

Whatever the expression, if our hearts are truly glorifying God then it's important to not judge the expression of others, or to feel guilty when our expression of worship doesn't look like that of others. In some Christian cultures, if you raise your hands during corporate worship in church, you're ostentatious. In other Christian cultures, if you don't raise your hands during corporate worship in church, you're stodgy and dull. If you clap your hands to the music, you're too enthusiastic. If you don't clap your hands, you're not cool. Remember that worship is the way we live and the words that proceed from our mouth. The expression of worship doesn't consist of a raised hand or bent knee. It has absolutely nothing to do with posture. Posture may help us to get into the proper attitude of worship by helping us focus, or by reminding us of our humble estate, but it's not in itself an expression of a worshipful heart. Much more important is that we express our celebration of God's glory in humility at the foot of His throne. This can be in the car on our way to work, in a conversation, or during a quiet time. It can happen while we're jogging, belting it out with the radio, gardening, or at other times.

Regardless of the manner of your expression, let's be faithful to follow to "continually offer up a sacrifice of praise to God, that is, the fruit of our lips acknowledging His name" (Hebrews 13:15).

Selah

You are my hiding place; you protect me from distress. You surround me with shouts of joy from those celebrating deliverance.
(Psalm 32:7)

Immortal, invisible, God only wise, In light inaccessible, hid from our eyes, Most blessed, most glorious, the Ancient of Days, Almighty, victorious, Thy great name we praise.

Great Father of glory, pure Father of light, Thine angels adore Thee, all veiling their sight; All praise we would render; oh, help us to see 'Tis only the splendor of light hideth Thee.
(Walter C. Smith)

Worship Is a Response

Worship robots—that's what we all tend toward. I've seen worship as merely a task: *I must worship in prayer. God is good, God is love, God is good, God is love.*

But worship is completely useless if it's mechanical. We can't separate a conscious awareness of God's glory from our worship. While that probably sounds obvious, isn't it true that we often try to make this separation? We think, "Oh, I need to worship as part of my prayer time," but that worship is contrived. We completely miss the beauty of worship when we offer it in empty words or in songs without heart. If we're distracted or unengaged, our worship is no better than that of the pagan who's worshiping only because he thinks he might somehow benefit from it.

One of the ways that our worship differs from that of other religions (besides that we worship the one true God) is that we worship from personal relationship with our God. He has saved us, now and forevermore. There's nothing that can separate us from His love, so we worship Him in response, rather than in effort to gain His approval.

As A. W. Tozer wrote:

> God has provided His salvation that we, individually and personally, might be vibrant children of God, loving God with all our hearts and worshiping Him in the beauty of holiness.

True worship can only be a response. We don't have the desire to worship Him unless He draws us to Himself and saves us. We don't have the wisdom to know God's attributes unless He reveals this to us through His Word. We don't know His beauty unless He reveals it to us through creation, poetry, music, and art.

It's a huge mistake to think we can stumble into God's throne room and offer up distracted or self-willed worship. Recall the account of Cain and Abel. We're told in Hebrews 11 that Abel offered his sacrifice in faith to God. But faith in what? Abel's faith was in God's promise to forgive his sin through that sacrifice, and ultimately through the perfect sacrifice of Jesus. Meanwhile, Cain offered a self-willed sacrifice when he brought an offering of produce from the field to offer the Lord. There was no blood to atone for his sins. He went on his own script of worship—either mindless, heartless, or both. He wasn't offering his sacrifice in response to God's promise of redemption. It's impossible to say whether he was belligerent or careless (both dangerous sins) with His offering. Whatever the case, the Lord was not pleased with him.

Perhaps we offer mindless or heartless worship because we don't look or listen for God. It's hard to respond to someone we don't see or hear. This isn't God's fault. He's continuously broadcasting His glory to the whole world through His creation, and to all believers through His Spirit and Word. The Spirit is always ready to flood our hearts with light to illuminate the spiritual world. Yet we've convinced ourselves in Christianity that busier is better, and we've settled for noise above the whispers and shouts of God's revealed glory to us.

If our time in the Word is distracted, we won't hear from the Lord. If we're too fascinated with modernity to look for His working in our lives and in the world, we won't see Him. Or perhaps we hear and see Him, but we're dull of senses and too brutish to give Him glory.

A vision-impaired man is unimpressed by the most spectacular display of colors. Only when we see—with keen acuity—God's vivid attributes and bright glory will we be able to respond to Him in worship. Let's pray that the Lord will grant us to see the intensity and many shades of His character, so we can respond with resounding worship that is both heartfelt and mindful.

Study Questions

1. What aspect of worship discussed in this chapter (or otherwise) do you struggle with most?

2. To help us in our worship of God, how do we rely on the working together of our mind, will, emotions, and spirit?

3. Read Psalm 98. What main characteristics of worship do you find there?

Chapter 3
Where Worship Fits In

Before time began, before the canvas of the universe was stretched out to display His glory, God was. He existed from eternity past in three distinct persons, the Father, the Son, and the Holy Spirit. There was perfect unity and love shared among the Persons of the Godhead, and they glorified each other in the splendor of deity. They were completely satisfied in their love and adoration of each other, needing nothing and no other being.

When time began, the angels and spiritual beings were created, some primarily as messengers and others primarily as worshipers. Although all spiritual beings were created with the privilege of experiencing God's glory and worshiping before His throne, the six-winged seraphim in particular never cease to worship the Lord, continuously crying "Holy, holy, holy."

One of the most prominent angels, Lucifer, wanted the worship and glory for himself. He became consumed by his magnificence and aspired to exalt himself above God to receive the worship of which God alone was worthy. Lucifer was instead cast out of heaven.

When God spoke to create the universe, the angels sang for joy in worship. The scroll of the universe was stretched out to show God's many attributes—His power, creativity, sovereignty, love, organization, omniscience, and eternality, among many others. The council of deity then planned the masterpiece, the crowning glory of creation: mankind. God formed man in His own image from the dust of the ground, and breathed life into him. Man would be given the indescribable gift of enjoying God's glorious presence in worship and intimacy.

But Lucifer—now Satan the adversary—made plans to derail this worship and intimacy. Although he desired worship, his weapon of choice against man was to tempt him toward self-worship, the same downfall as his own. Telling Eve that she could become like God, Satan dared her to rebel and try her hand at deification.

Adam and Eve both fell into disobedience, and plunged mankind into rebellion against God and separation from Him. By rebelling against God and following the original rebel, they became his spiritual progeny. And we, by both choice and pedigree, have joined Adam, Eve, and Satan in the rebellion against God and the worship of self—a rebellion that has destined us for eternity in fire, judgment, and separation from the holy God.

But God, rich in mercy and forgiveness, still desired that we could experience His glory in worship and intimacy. So in keeping with His perfect justice, He sent Jesus His Son to earth to live as one of us and to serve our sentence. As God in human flesh, Jesus lived a perfect life. Motivated by His love for the Father and His love for us, Jesus died on a cross for us, the just for the unjust. He took God's holy judgment on Himself so that we could be seen as righteous before God. He then conquered death in a physical resurrection so that we can be assured of our resurrection with Him. Because of the Father's love for the Son and His love for His newly redeemed people, He will exalt the name of Jesus above all names.

The salvation that Jesus provides for us has three parts, and worship is integral to each of them. The appropriation of salvation— sometimes called justification—involves a realization of God's holiness and how we've utterly missed His holy standard. When we realize this, we fall to our knees before His throne and ask for His forgiveness and mercy, trusting in Christ as the Savior of our sins. Thus starts our spiritual life—in humility and worship of His holiness, love, mercy, and sufficiency of Christ's sacrifice. We exchange the worship of self for the worship of God.

As we continue our spiritual relationship with God, the second part of our salvation is known as sanctification. During this process, God continues to impress upon us the details of His character, both from the teaching of His Word, the Bible, and through a life of experience in walking with God. In this process of sanctification, whenever we fail to obey God and He forgives us according to His promises, we ought to humbly worship Him for His faithfulness. When He gives us joy in His presence, we ought to sing praises to Him.

The final part of our salvation can be called glorification, as the presence of sin will be taken from us and our relationship with God will be restored to its original intent in worship and intimacy. When those who've been justified are taken up to be with the Lord in heaven, we'll see God in the splendor of His glory and fall at His feet in worship, enraptured by His presence and joining in song with the angels who've been worshiping since the beginning of time.

His Glory

This life of ours is all about God's glory.

When we glorify God, we're fulfilling God's plan for our lives. The first time we truly glorify God is at the time of salvation. It's when we humbly admit that we're sinners and that we've violated the laws of a holy God. We also exalt God's holiness, His love for us, His mercy, and the sufficiency of His sacrifice for the forgiveness of sins. After our coming to salvation, whenever we glorify God to Him, it's worship.

Meanwhile, whenever we glorify God to unbelievers, we're witnessing. Our focus in witnessing to others should not only be the technical steps of becoming a believer. It should be God's glory and our humble estate—the same focus that brought us to faith. Unfortunately, when we don't witness to others, it's because we're more concerned about our glory than God's glory. We don't want to be embarrassed or thought of as unprofessional. But when we're consumed with God's glory, those things don't matter to us and we share His glory with all those around us.

When we glorify God to believers, it's fellowship. And when we glorify God for eternity, it's glorification.

In our walk with God, our glorification of God through worship is essential for the other spiritual disciplines to be of value. Study of the Bible without worship is, at best, attempted self-improvement. Prayer without worship is a soliloquy. Scripture memory without worship is an exercise.

So then, worship is foundational to the biblical fundamentals which build God's kingdom where His glory resides. Don't think that your spiritual life can thrive without worship. It can't. This world and all that is in it is meant for worship.

Selah

Who is a God like you?

Who forgives sin and pardons the rebellion of those who remain among his people?

Who does not stay angry forever, but delights in showing loyal love.

Who will once again have mercy on us?

Who will conquer our evil deeds?

Who will hurl our sins into the depths of the sea? (Micah 7:18-19)

Almighty and everlasting God, in whose hands are life and death, by whose will all things were created, and by whose providence they are sustained, I return Thee thanks that Thou hast given me life, and that Thou hast continued it to this time; that Thou hast hitherto forborne to snatch me away in the midst of sin and folly, and hast permitted me still to enjoy the means of grace, and vouchsafed to call me yet again to repentance. Grant, O merciful Lord, that Thy call may not be vain; that my life may not be continued to increase my guilt, and that Thy gracious forbearance may not harden my heart in wickedness. (New Year's prayer by Samuel Johnson)

So Who Cares?

Since we were created for worship, worship doesn't go unnoticed by the evil one. Throughout the pages of Scripture, we're told of his lust for worship. Nearly every encounter in Scripture points to his insatiable desire to supplant God and gain worship. Causing his fall, he desired to ascend above the stars of God and sit enthroned on the assembly (Isaiah 14:13). Do those in the assembly know how valuable their worship is? Do we know how valuable our worship is and how cosmically desperate Satan is to obtain it?

In the garden of Eden, Satan sets himself up as the benevolent provider and protector (Genesis 3:4-5). Since the creation of man, God has been the believer's Abba Father, our Provider and Protector, for which we worship Him. In Eden, Satan was blatantly attempting to steal this role—and our worship.

In Job 1, we're given a view of heaven and a dialogue between God and Satan. God declares how Job is pure, upright, a God-fearer, and one who turns away from evil. Satan doesn't seem to mind that Job is pure, upright, and one who turns away from evil. Instead he jumps on Job's fear of God, which is the wellspring of worship. The challenge is not to lure Job away into adultery, thievery, anger, or greed. Satan's desired result is to change Job's worship of God into cursing of God. Worship is the issue.

When Satan tempts Christ in the wilderness, the final assault is his offering Christ all the kingdoms of the earth for Christ's worship.

Think about the ramifications of this for a second. If Christ had done this, then earth in the present would basically be heaven. Christ would have likely banished Satan from this realm. He would have restored justice and mercy. This world would no longer be defined by physical and emotional suffering. There would be no paradigm of murder, starvation, adultery, broken homes, addictions, sex trafficking, or other vices. We would be living in paradise. Satan doesn't fear the social gospel. However, Christ would have been sacrificing His sacrifice for us. The gospel would no longer be. There would be no means of making rebels into worshipers. We would perish in our sins and sin natures, even though this life would be a happy one.

In *Tempted and Tried,* Russell Moore writes the following about Christ's third temptation:

> The Devil doesn't mind "family values" as long as what you ultimately value is the family. Satan doesn't mind "social justice" as long as you see justice as most importantly social... Churches, Satan doesn't care if your people vote for pro-life candidates, stay married, have sex with whom they're supposed to, and tear up at all the praise choruses, as long as they don't see the only power that cancels condemnation—the gospel of Christ crucified. Satan so fears that gospel, he was willing to surrender his entire empire just to stave it off. He still is.

Satan and Christ both had their sights set much higher—on an eternity of our worship of God. And Christ won in a shutout.

At the very end of history, we see Satan thrown down from heaven in Revelation 12. When he cannot get the worship he craves above the earth, or successfully accuse worshipers in heaven, he basks in all the worship he can muster on earth, and he tries to devour all who won't worship him.

Make no mistake, Satan is all about your worship, and his insatiable lust doesn't begin in the end times. It affects you every day in the things you see, hear, touch, and taste. He'll dangle trinkets around you and tempt you to infatuation, hoping that you forget your purpose and future. If Satan cannot have your worship, he'll make every attempt to derail your worship of God.

With a glorious eternity ahead of us, as promised by God, how can we give in to Satan's wiles, speaking with other believers primarily about investment returns, TV shows, hobbies, or people, rather than the glorious riches of Christ?

Reality versus Higher Reality

Individuals who aren't part of God's redemptive plan don't believe that this life is all about God's glory. This is because they haven't had their spiritual eyes opened to see God's glory and His love for them in light of their baseness. Those of us who've tasted God's goodness to us in salvation, but who don't worship Him as we should, have accepted this world's reality as a substitute for God's higher reality. Our five senses tell us that what we experience in the flesh here is more substantial than the higher spiritual reality. That's why we often pray a Scripture verse back to God in worship, then lose focus as our mind wanders to the good movie we saw last night. It's why we think about our to-do list as we mouth the lyrics of a hymn. It's why we evaluate other people during the church service rather than focusing on God. We act as though this fleshly reality is more real than the higher spiritual reality.

In 2 Kings 6, we read of Elisha and his servant and the Syrian army. Elisha had been warning the king of Israel about where the Syrians would attack him, so the king of Syria sent an army to take out Elisha. When the army appeared, Elisha's servant began to panic: "Oh no, my master! What will we do?" (6:15). The threat was real.

But there's a higher reality. Elisha prayed that the eyes of his servant would be opened to the higher spiritual reality. Immediately, the servant saw that Elisha was correct when he said, "Don't be afraid, for our side outnumbers them." He saw that Elisha was surrounded by horses and chariots of fire. The higher reality, though not normally seen, will trump the reality we experience with our senses. Interestingly, Elisha prayed for the Syrian's physical eyes to be blinded—for their preservation, so the Syrians didn't attack in the presence of the fiery angels.

Similarly, in Numbers 22, we read the account of Balaam and his much more spiritual donkey. After a conversation with his donkey that was presumably strange, the Lord opened up Balaam's eyes to see the spiritual reality. There was the angel of the Lord standing before him, causing him to fall to the ground.

We, of course, don't need to be surrounded by fiery chariots or rebuked by donkeys to be able to see a spiritual ultra-reality instead of only our physical reality. We rarely take notice of the daytime or nighttime sky, yet in the spiritual higher reality, the sky is constantly declaring the glory of God (Psalm 19:1). We resent that individual who wronged us, but the spiritual reality is that this person is being used by God for God's purposes; he's loved by God and is being wooed by His Spirit just as we are. Or we envy those who're successful in the world, when the higher spiritual reality is that the blessing of relationship with Christ in this life (not even counting the next) is more enriching than anything the world has to offer.

Do you see this? Do you believe it?

In John 9, one man's spiritual eyes were opened, and the spiritual eyes of a group of men were left blind. This chapter tells of how Jesus healed a blind man. Notice that after the disciples questioned Jesus about who had sinned to make this man blind, Jesus relayed to them the higher reality—that the man was blind for the glory of God. Now, if you were that blind man, you might have wondered why a loving God would make you blind just for His glory. You might wonder why it took so many years for Jesus to find and heal him for His glory. Certainly, during the many years of blindness when he didn't know his ailment was for the glory of God, he must have thought life had dealt him an unfair and cruel blow. These were unpleasant years of disability and humiliation, with many people walking by, as the disciples did, and surmising that this man had received what he deserved. However, this man—with spiritual eyes partially opened—knew of a higher reality. He gave witness to Christ's work, and although not knowing exactly who Jesus was, he knew that He was from God. Then his spiritual eyes were fully opened; he believed and worshiped.

The Pharisees in this account were left spiritually blind to the higher reality. They knew only the physical words on the physical page of the law as they worshiped their own spiritual agendas. They could not accept that Jesus might be the Christ sent from God, because He didn't match their perception of who God ought to be. Jesus gave sad commentary on how their spiritual eyes were blind because they didn't see the higher reality of their sin and their need for a Savior. Had they worshiped Christ alongside the blind man with partial understanding of the higher spiritual reality, Christ would have fully opened their eyes to see His glory and deity.

Oh, that the eyes of our heart would be opened to the spiritual higher reality! That when we worship, we would see the greatness of our God in His majestic splendor, rather than our agendas or the physical distractions around us. If we could be more aware of the constant worship around us emanating from creation and the angels, we wouldn't zone out after three minutes of worship.

Let this be our prayer—that our eyes would be open to the spiritual reality of His greatness. And that His purpose in creating us would be fulfilled in us as worshipers.

Study Questions

1. Expressed worship of God is inextricably linked to justification and glorification. Why do we see it as an optional part of sanctification (aside from this being "just our sin nature")?

2. Study Numbers 22:21-38. What are the dangers of believers seeing only the physical reality before them? What is the result of spiritual eye-opening?

3. Describe how a scenario might play out in your experience today or tomorrow as you choose to see the spiritual higher reality, rather than only the physical reality.

4. What spiritual higher reality do you want to be most assured of in your walk with the Lord? What physical realities in your life do you need to look past to see this?

Chapter 4
Singing the Praises of His Praise

I thought I was a smart kid. I'm sure I wasn't any smarter than any other kid enrolled in the Sunday school program of our conservative evangelical church, but I thought I was pretty smart nonetheless. I quickly learned that with a repertoire of three answers, I could be the first to raise my hand to answer nearly any question accurately without even hearing the entire question. For instance:

> "What is the problem with...?"
>
> My hand would shoot up in the air as I blurted out, "Sin!"
>
> "What are some ways that we can grow...?"
>
> I'd say, "Read your Bible and pray!"
>
> "Who can...?"
>
> "God!" I'd answer.

Attending a strong Bible-teaching church—where it was an egregious offense for even the very young to be ignorant of the roles of the Trinity—I was occasionally corrected on that last answer. "No, not God—it's Jesus." So anytime the question cued an answer relating to the Godhead, I would shout out "God and Jesus," covering at least two-thirds of my base without even thinking about the profundity of question or answer.

Although I laugh at my six-year-old Sunday school conquests, I've found that we all tend to answer spiritual questions in life with rubber stamp answers that have become automatic. Cerebrally, we can answer nearly every question posed to us about the spiritual life. Usually they're good answers based in Scripture, but they become over-simplified when we skip thinking about the worth, depth, and value behind each answer.

If asked why we're to implement worship into our prayer life and conversations, we might be tempted to raise our hand and blurt out, "Because the Bible tells us to!" This is true, and our most important reason to worship is for God's glory and His pleasure. But there are many benefits to our own spiritual lives from integrating vocalized worship into our spiritual lifestyle.

This is the beauty of God's commands to us from Scripture. When we obey His commands, not only do we please Him and lay up heavenly treasures, but we also benefit from that obedience here on earth. God's Word is our instruction manual for navigating this life successfully. Obedience brings not only blessing from God but a perfectly satisfactory life experience that can be obtained in no other way. God is so gracious to make His commands spiritually delectable *and* nutritious. Although worship is a spiritual discipline, it's also a joy.

So aside from the chief purpose of worship in bringing glory to God, let's look at some ways that worship enriches our lives.

Worship Brings Vibrancy to Our Lives

I recently finished a book by a well-known Christian author about the spiritual disciplines. It was a great book that I would highly recommend to all. However, a passage on the discipline of prayer caught my attention. The author contrasted quick, spontaneous prayer with long, scheduled prayer. Quick and spontaneous prayers, the author said, are important for time-of-need supplications (such as witnessing), whereas long and scheduled prayers are beneficial for confessing sins and asking for strength to overcome habitual sins. Although these are essential parts of prayer and our spiritual walk, I became weary imagining a prayer life devoted solely to supplication and confession. *Where's the part where we delight in the Lord?* I asked myself.

Every person is looking for a more vibrant life. All our idols promise that they'll give us a more exciting and meaningful life. We constantly seek things to give us a more vibrant life. Marketing specialists are well aware of this, and nearly every advertisement tries to prove that their product can give you that more vibrant life—which may be why funeral homes rarely buy Super Bowl commercial slots.

The worship of God brings vibrancy into our lives to an extent that nothing else can. When we see His attributes such as love or power displayed in our book or movie characters, we're drawn to these characters because they fascinate us. In a superhero tale, the observer is drawn into the familiar but captivating plot of good versus evil. All seems right when the powerful and virtuous character dominates the forces of evil. I finish these tales feeling inspired to hit the gym and being on the lookout for persons needing a rescue from supervillains—or in my more realistic world, rescuing my wife from a cockroach in the living room. The power displayed by these superheroes is nearly always exaggerated from what's possible in reality, but that doesn't lessen the delight taken in these movies.

Some may find chick flicks more captivating than superhero movies. The warm and tingly feeling that washes over them as love conquers all is a powerful feeling that keeps people going back to watch more chick flicks. Subconsciously, there's a desire to love and be loved in the way that's portrayed on the pages or screen, no matter how artificial the love and the scenarios might be.

However, these imperfect portrayals are mere shadows of God's perfect themes. You want a superhero? Read the pages of Scripture to see God's transcendental supremacy throughout time past and future. There's no greater warrior, real or imagined. You want a love story? Read about God's love for the Persons of the Trinity and for us. There has never been a story written that's so full of passion and selflessness.

Worship allows us to explore, celebrate, and emulate all of God's perfect attributes, the relishing of which adds zest to our prayer life. Even better is knowing that we're on His winning side and that all His attributes settle cosmic events for our favor. We're living out the greatest drama imaginable, and we're on the winning side with a Captain who's unfathomably supreme!

In our prayer lives, delighting in the Lord comes from both worship and thanksgiving.

Consider how Psalm 147 begins:

> *Praise the Lord!* For it is good to sing praises to our God! Yes, praise is pleasant and appropriate!

Note that the psalmist doesn't say praise is our duty or our struggle, but rather that it's *pleasant.* If you've had a tough day at work, try singing a hymn on your way home. It really is pleasant, and will help to change your mood. If you're depressed, spend fifteen minutes praising God's care and love for you. If you're worried, take time to worship God's sovereignty in all situations.

Worship is not only good; it's also enriching for the soul. We do have duties, disciplines, and struggles in our faith, and at times worship *is* a duty and discipline. But if we forget about the joy of worship, our spiritual lives are in danger of drying up.

Unfortunately, some might associate this dried-up spiritual life with the Puritans. But one of the great Puritan theologians, John Owen, said this about delighting in worship:

> This delight in the worship of God, so much commended in the Scripture, and proposed unto our

example, consists not in any carnal self-pleasing, or satisfaction in the outward modes or manner of the performance of divine worship; but it is a holy, soul-refreshing contemplation on the will, wisdom, grace, and condescension of God, in that he is pleased, of his own sovereign mere will and grace, so to manifest himself unto such poor sinful creatures as we are, so to condescend unto our weakness, so to communicate himself unto us, so to excite and draw forth our souls unto himself, and to give us such pledges of his gracious intercourse with us by Jesus Christ. By the contemplation of these things is the soul drawn forth to delight in God.

Delighting in the worship of the Lord leads to a vibrant spiritual life. In nature, vibrancy attracts. Think of a vibrant flower. Birds, butterflies, bees, and humans are all drawn to it. The flower isn't trying to be overly beautiful; it's living its intended vibrant life as it drinks in sunshine, water, and soil nutrients, and then lives out its design. Similarly in our spiritual lives, we're designed for vibrancy as we take in God's Word and delight in His character through worship. Without this, our spiritual lives will be grayscale or monochromatic. However, with the vibrancy that worshipful delight brings, we become attractive to believers and unbelievers alike, drawing them in to become partakers of that same vibrant life and to drink more deeply in His worship.

Worship Brings Humility

That didn't hurt! Oh, how much like children we tend to be as God's people! I often hear stories of children, usually boys, who after being disciplined will turn around and tell their parent, "That didn't hurt." Of course, what follows is typically much better remembered by the child. Little do children realize that discipline is meant to bring them to humility and repentance, not for them to prove how tough they are.

Many of us are familiar with God's discipline in our lives through various trials and the consequences of our actions. Ideally, we learn the extent of our sinful flesh, our strong will, and our need for Him. His discipline is a wonderful gift as He graciously but pointedly teaches us full surrender to Him. There are few greater joys in life than to realize our insufficiency and His sufficiency, because this realization stills the struggle of our striving for sufficiency that accompanies many to the grave.

When we're not aligned with God's will and we're not in a good place spiritually, His discipline can evoke responses of pride and self-sufficiency: "That didn't hurt," or "I can do better." But if we respond correctly, these trials and chastisements will ultimately bring us to humility and sanctification.

Thankfully, there's an alternate way of learning humility apart from getting it beaten into us. A better path is to habitually enter into the Lord's presence through worship. The very heart of worship must be humility, and true worship will humble us further. When we celebrate God's perfection, our baseness becomes glaring. We're brought low in humility and quickly realize that our rightful place is at His footstool. His love and benevolence humble us further as we try to grasp how He can love us so much. Why is He faithful to us when we're so utterly unworthy? Although we're blinded by the glare of our humble estate in His presence, we can take joy in His perfection. What a pleasant way to cultivate humility in our lives!

Selah

For you are a protector for the poor, a protector for the needy in their distress, a shelter from the rainstorm, a shade from the heat.
(Isaiah 25:4)

Wonderful merciful Savior, Precious redeemer and friend, Who would have thought that a lamb could

Rescue the souls of men, Oh, You rescue the souls of men.

Counselor, comforter, keeper, Spirit we long to embrace, You offer hope when our hearts have Hopelessly lost the way, Oh, we hopelessly lost the way.

You are the One that we praise, You are the One we adore, You give the healing and grace our Hearts always hunger for, Oh, our hearts always hunger for.

Almighty infinite Father, Faithfully loving Your own, Here in our weakness You find us, Falling before Your throne,

Oh, we're falling before Your throne.
(Dawn Rodgers and Eric Wyse)

Worship Helps Us Accept God's Will

We sometimes focus our attention on "big" sins and congratulate ourselves that we're not convicted murderers, adulterers, or thieves. But some of the "small misdemeanors" that are most often overlooked include placing our will as more important than God's. The obvious outworking of this is complaining, and the less visible form is anxiety.

Check yourself. In any situation that isn't exactly as we intended, most of us have an uncanny ability to extract something negative from it to complain about. How easy it is to let slip words that undermine our faith in God's sovereignty and omnipotence! Complaining is nothing less than asserting that we could be running things better than God does.

Or maybe the struggle is anxiety. There may be a situation that causes you to feel out of control, and the more you think about it, the more you can't stop thinking about it. You know such anxiety is faithlessness, yet you feel incapable of overcoming it. Every rational consideration that you manufacture against the source of anxiety gets drowned in the sea of overwhelming thoughts. The fear of the object grips you much more than the fear of the Lord, even when you know it shouldn't be this way. The anxiety even hijacks your body and causes sleeplessness, substance addiction, and isolationist tendencies, all of which compound the anxiety.

You may find yourself angry toward God for putting you in this situation, or for not immediately removing whatever's causing your anxiety. Even though anxiety can be a physical condition and require medical treatment, there are times when an unwell spiritual life allows it to cripple us. When this is the case, anxiety shows a lack of faith and submission to God's will.

One of the most difficult things in our walk with God is to accept His will when it's not in line with our own. "Bad situations," we call them. If we're not completely focused on God's love, omnipotence, omniscience, faithfulness, and sovereignty, we'll find ourselves on the complaining-anxiety spectrum when undesirable things happen. Of course, we know from Romans 8:28 that "God causes all things to work together for good to those who love God, to those who are called according to *His* purpose," but that wonderful nugget of wisdom often stays in our head and doesn't make it into our heart. This verse in the context of unpleasant circumstances is like an oxygen mask dangling in front of us on a plane that has lost cabin pressure. All we need to do put on the mask and breathe—or face the consequences of suffocation. Oftentimes, we choose to suffocate while complaining or fretting bitterly about it.

Consider this interrogation for God's people given through the prophet Malachi:

> *A son* naturally honors his father and a slave respects his master. If I am your father, where is my honor? If I am your master, where is my respect? The LORD who rules over all asks you this, you priests who make light of my name! But you reply, "How have we made light of your name?" You

*are offering improper sacrifices on my altar, yet you ask,
"How have we offended you?" By treating the table of the
LORD as if it is of no importance!* (Malachi 1:6-7)

When we choose to complain rather than worship, we ought to
hear resounding in our spirits these personalized versions of that
passage:

"You sing about My power on Sunday; why don't you
trust that I'm in control of this situation?"

"You sing about My love; why do you think the
situation I'm allowing you to go through is truly bad
for you?"

"You sing about My omnipresence; why do you think
you're alone in what you're going through?"

"You sing about My justice; why do you think your
antagonists are escaping unnoticed?"

Oh, the conviction!

But how do we get Romans 8:28 from our heads into our heart so
that we understand and accept God's will for our lives, no matter how
bad it may seem to our finite minds? How do we stop the
complaining before it jumps out of our mouth? How do we break the
crushing cycles of anxiety?

We do it by focusing on God's glory. There's no better cure for
complaining or for anxiety. The deeper we know the Lord, the more
we can rest in His attributes.

Worship is a joyful and confident expression of faith in who God
is. It helps us freely admit that we indeed are *not* in control of the
situation, and it reminds us that the One who is in control is kind and
just. It fills our mind with His glory and crowds out the intrusive

thoughts of faithlessness from our minds. We begin to see situations in the light of His perfect character, realizing that His will is always good.

This is the process through which the Holy Spirit bends our will to conform to God's. As we renew our minds and spirits with the worship of His character, the asphyxiating pollution of complaining and anxious obsessions gives way to the refreshing glory of the Lord, giving us life and breath again.

Paul had discovered this when he wrote of his desire "that with complete boldness, even now as always, Christ will be exalted in my body, whether I live or die" (Philippians 1:20). What a freeing mindset, to leave life or death in God's hands so He can choose which would glorify Him more! As the infinite facets of God's character become more understood by our minds and hearts, we want nothing more than for His greatness to be spread throughout all the earth by whatever means necessary.

This mindset was shown to me when my mother was diagnosed with advanced-stage ovarian cancer. She was otherwise completely healthy, and the diagnosis was a bitter shock to us. A few days after her surgery, she told me she was thankful she had cancer.

"That's a godly attitude," I told her. "To be thankful to God despite the cancer."

"No," she said, "I'm thankful to God *for* the cancer."

I redirected my thinking. *She must be thanking God for the patience and other fruit that the trial of cancer will bring.* But I was wrong again.

She went on to explain that this cancer had already given her the opportunity to share the gospel with many doctors and nurses whom she would otherwise have been unable to reach.

My mind reeled. I'd been having a difficult time accepting the Lord's will for her in the matter. By God's grace, however, her will was so neatly lined up with God's will that she saw only His goodness to her: He had sovereignly allowed her to get cancer so she could spread His glory in places where she previously had no access. During her entire treatment of chemotherapy, she never wavered in her worship of God's goodness and mercy, both privately and to others. She took every opportunity to share God's love with the doctors, nurses, and patients she met. Just as the entire praetorian guard learned of God's glory because of Paul's unwavering testimony (Philippians 1:13), so everyone my mom came across in the hospital knew the reason for her cancer. A perspective such as hers comes only from a lifetime of adoring and worshiping God.

In difficult circumstances, worship shifts us from asking "Why?" to confidently exclaiming, "Because *God*…!" When bad situations or anxiety tap us on the shoulder, a worshiping heart gives a shush. "Don't you see the greatness of the Lord?"

There's no room for complaining or anxiety in the worshiping heart. This is because the overflow there of God's attributes will leave no doubt that He's in control, that His plan is good, and that His kingdom is infinitely more grand than ours. It's from this perspective that Job offered his famous statement: "Even if he slays me, I will hope in him" (Job 13:15).

God has great things in store for us that are much bigger than happiness and worldly success. Those greater things are His plan.

Worship Prepares Us for Our Future

A few years ago, I got a phone call with a request for me to play violin at a private dinner party for a magistrate from an Asian country. I'd played for important people before, but only a few as prominent as this man.

Immediately after hanging up the phone, I researched this man I would be meeting. What city was he from? What was his relationship to the US? What was his religion? There was absolutely no way I was going to meet him and ask, "So who are you?" Not only did I research him and all his characteristics, but I also practiced for the occasion, which I rarely did for background dinner music. I'd played for hundreds of dinner parties and considered them easy.

It was a good thing that I practiced. This man turned out to be a classical music aficionado. He turned forty-five minutes of the party into a personal concert for him, asking me to play his favorite selections of some of the toughest violin repertoire.

Think of the numerous celebrity-fan interactions that have become comically famous because of the outlandish adoration displayed by fans when meeting a celebrity. Quite often people lose their minds in such a situation, all because of their perception of the famous person's importance (real or imagined). Certainly, one would never purposefully enter such an encounter with a celebrity without preparing for it—in what to wear, what to say, and what impression to try and make.

How much more should we prepare for our future face-to-face meeting with God and our worship of Him in heaven! Compared to His greatness, earthly dignitaries and celebrities are as dust. Although our ability to know God on this side of heaven is veiled before our faith gives way to sight, we desire that our frail minds should seek to comprehend every facet of His character. Our worship here on earth helps us to know and practice well the eternal songs awaiting us.

Throughout the book of Revelation, we read about the ceaseless worship of God and our future participation. However, we tend to be severely nearsighted in our present lives. We schedule for temporal advantage only, and we do little to know or enjoy our eternal life. Perhaps we think that our worshiping of Him in heaven will be "mindless background music." But in reality, we'll be singing to Him and glorifying Him in the presence of His very person. Preparation matters!

As we prepare for the next life by learning God's attributes and reflexively praising Him, we begin to fulfill the purpose for which we were created—to be perfected on the other side of physical death. If you aren't already excited about our glorious future in heaven, here's a snapshot:

Then a voice came from the throne, saying: "Praise our God all you his servants, and all you who fear Him, both the small and the great!" Then I heard what sounded like the voice of a vast throng, like the roar of many waters and like loud crashes of thunder. They were shouting: "Hallelujah! For the Lord our God, the All-Powerful, reigns! Let us rejoice and exult and give him glory, because the wedding celebration of the Lamb has come, and his bride has made herself ready." (Revelation 19:5-7)

On the subject of physical death, our preparation for our worship-filled future eases our fears of death. One who's consistently enraptured by the worship of the King of the universe understands what joy there is in this adulatory communion, even amid the sorrows and blemishes of this life. Our soul—in anticipation of the day when sin's deceit no longer distorts our understanding, and our imperfect faith no longer veils our eyes to God's glory—will rejoice at the prospect of seeing God as He is.

Such trials show the proven character of your faith, which is much more valuable than gold—gold that is tested by fire, even though it is passing away—and will bring praise and glory and honor when Jesus Christ is revealed. You have not seen him, but you love him. You do not see him now but you believe in him, and so you rejoice with an indescribable and glorious joy, because you are attaining the goal of your faith—the salvation of your souls. (1 Peter 1:7-9)

What joy it will be when our faith becomes sight, and our worship will be uninhibited as we're overwhelmed by His presence! That joy is waiting for us on the other side of physical death. Worship here in this life is our appetizer, readying us with eager anticipation of what's to come.

Study Questions

1. Besides worship, what are some ways Scripture teaches us to bring vibrancy into our spiritual lives?

2. Is spiritual vibrancy through worship easier to cultivate in easy or difficult times? Why?

3. Read James 5:7-11, where we're told that Job was steadfast in his suffering. What are some characteristics from the passage of someone who has accepted God's will in steadfastness?

4. Are you concerned that an eternity of worship in heaven might be boring? Why or why not?

5. Read Revelation 4:8-11; 5:12-14; 7:10-12; 11:16-18; 14:6-7; 15:3-4; and 19:1-6. Why are all these actual words of worship recorded for us, rather than just a statement that some particular person or group "worshiped God"?

Chapter 5
Worship and Sanctification

Gone are the days of the butcher, baker, and candlestick maker. These specialty stores have been replaced by supermarkets and web-based marketplaces, where you can get everything you want at one place. With apologies to those who prefer butchers, bakers, and candlestick makers, worship is the supermarket of godly disciplines and attributes. Any area of Christlikeness that you wish to cultivate in your life can be brought about through worship.

This isn't to minimize the importance of other disciplines of the faith, but rather to emphasize the centrality of worship to the Christian life. Cheerful, sacrificial giving is essential for the Christian walk and produces great joy, but it doesn't obviously cultivate holiness. Serving helps us grow in humility and obedience, but it doesn't necessarily cultivate righteousness. Worship will help us to cultivate all the virtues while also bringing us into sanctification, or Christlikeness. This is because worship is our transformative gazing upon Christ, along with reflexive rejoicing.

Joni Eareckson Tada expresses it this way:

> God knows that the more we focus on Him—praising and blessing Him; musing and meditating on His beauty and graces—we are changed. We become that which captures our emotional, intellectual, and willful focus. Do we want to be more loving? Consider the

loveliness of Christ and meditate on that—it'll change you. Do we want to be more holy? Focus on the Father's disdain for sin and His goodness and purity—it'll change you. Do we want our hearts to be devoted to God and adoring of Him? Ask the Spirit to reveal the glory of the Godhead and how utterly captivating God is—you'll fall in love with the Lord. This is how God is glorified!

Sanctification is the goal of our salvation here on earth. Too often, we think of sanctification as abstaining from sin. Although that's certainly part of it, sanctification is so much more. Instead of loving adequately, sanctification is loving abundantly. Instead of administering grace, sanctification is lavishing it.

Sanctification is becoming Christlike in all areas, and from the time that we're saved, we should be on an all-out blitz to become more like Him. Initially, our state as a newborn believer is often not very Christlike. Finally, when we're glorified, we'll be like Christ, for we'll see Him just as He is (1 John 3:2). In the interim, we strive by the power of the Holy Spirit and the working of God in us to become more like Him. This happens when we realize our desperate need of Him and gaze upon Him through meditation on His Word and worship.

So the purpose of our worship is *not* that we avoid the sin of not worshiping. That would lead to the checklist mentality of checking a box every Sunday morning. Worship should rather be done continuously—in the blitz for sanctification.

The Lifeblood of Sanctification

Building on what we've covered about worship, two essentials of worship are first, realizing (in a spiritual reorientation) our baseness compared to His glory, and second, putting away idolatry, particularly self-worship. When we implement these two principles, we understand that worshiping God is our position in life, and it's the only thing that satisfies us.

In the process of sanctification, that realization becomes stronger, and we become less desperate for the things of the world and more desperate for God's glory. God's glory becomes like oxygen for our spiritual lives.

If we trace the path of oxygen from our breathing the air on through the process of metabolism in our bodies, we find a common theme: It's delivered to a tissue more desperate for oxygen than the one holding it. For instance, the air has a percentage of oxygen in it, and when taken into the lungs, that air diffuses through the alveolar walls and is bound by deoxygenated hemoglobin, which has more affinity for oxygen than the air does. In a typical individual, not all the hemoglobin is desaturated, therefore not all the hemoglobin receives oxygen. Once in the bloodstream, the oxygen has the opportunity to diffuse across capillary walls to oxygenate cells, but once again, only the cells that are desperate for the oxygen receive the transfer. This principle continues on the inside of the cell all the way through the entire process of metabolism.

If the hemoglobin is already bound by oxygen that hasn't been utilized, there'll be no transfer of oxygen to it. Worse, if an imitation of oxygen (such as carbon monoxide) binds to the hemoglobin but cannot be used by the organism's tissues, the organism will die.

The spiritual analogy is that realization of God's glory is imparted to us when we're desperate for it. This desperation originates in the acknowledgment of our lowliness against His greatness, and in our keeping ourselves from imitation gods which prevent us from worshiping the true God.

Elite athletes are able to train and perform at a level that most of us are physically unable to attain. They can deoxygenate their venous blood to a much greater degree than the general population. This, in addition to increased hemoglobin production, leads to much more oxygen transport across the membranes of the lungs. Likewise, as we grow in the process of sanctification, we're more aware of God's glory and more desperate for it than when we were spiritual couch potatoes.

Worship happens when our need for God's glory is met—when our spiritual tissues become oxygenated. A small awareness and desperation for His glory will result in little worship, just as a proper awareness and need will result in an abundance of worship. God is gracious to show us as much of His glory as we seek Him for— whether much or little.

Like carbon monoxide, idols can block us from being aware that we need God's glory. Hemoglobin that's bound by carbon monoxide merely waves to the oxygen molecule as it passes by, in the same way that we forsake being filled up by God's glory in worship if other things are holding our affections with more affinity. Like death by carbon monoxide, we'll die a slow spiritual death without realizing we're dying.

The cure for this spiritual ailment is similar to the physical one: removal of the offending agent, then flooding the system with the antidote. We must remove idols from our lives and flood our lives with the worship of God's glory.

Selah

The LORD's loyal kindness never ceases; his compassions never end. They are fresh every morning; your faithfulness is abundant!

"My portion is the LORD," I have said to myself, so I will put my hope in him.

The LORD is good to those who trust in him, to the one who seeks him. (Lamentations 3:22-25)

Great is Thy faithfulness, O God my Father, There is no shadow of turning with Thee; Thou changest not,

Thy compassions, they fail not As Thou hast been Thou forever wilt be.

Great is Thy faithfulness! Great is Thy faithfulness!

Morning by morning new mercies I see; All I have needed Thy hand hath provided—Great is Thy faithfulness," Lord, unto me! (Thomas Chisolm)

You are worthy, our Lord and God, to receive glory and honor and power, since you created all things, and because of your will they existed and were created! (Revelation 4:11)

Gazing upon Christ

True worship is the celebratory gaze upon Christ by His people. As twentieth-century evangelist Manley Beasley said, "A glimpse of God will save you. To gaze at Him will sanctify you."

Consequently, worship should develop our sanctification and bring us into Christ's likeness. But sometimes this doesn't seem to happen in our life. Why?

The key lies in the concept of gazing. This is more than the casual glance we often cast as we hurriedly spend time in the Word, then allow worldly distractions to cause us to forget what we've read. It's a constant and thorough examination that comes through memorization, meditation, and prayer. It's a focus similar to that of elite athletes that causes them to block out the crowds and competition.

The author of Hebrews speaks of this fixation on Jesus and the role it plays in our sanctification:

Therefore, since we are surrounded by such a great cloud of witnesses, we must get rid of every weight and the sin that clings so closely, and run with endurance the race set out for

> *us, keeping our eyes fixed on Jesus, the pioneer and perfecter*
> *of our faith. For the joy set out for him he endured the cross,*
> *disregarding its shame, and has taken his seat at the right*
> *hand of the throne of God.*
> (Hebrews 12:1-2)

The concepts of "gazing" and "fixing our eyes" denote a steadfast, thorough, and undistracted viewing. This is the advantage of worship in our everyday lives in addition to Sunday morning worship. On Sunday mornings, the songs come and go quickly. We may sense one line of the song speaking to us, but then we rapidly go to the next. Many times we're distracted by the cute baby two rows over, or the poor singing coming from the row behind us, or the weird hairdo in the row in front of us. The routine of singing familiar songs can also impede our ability to gaze intently upon Christ. When we worship in our quiet times, prayer times, or conversations, we're more able to eliminate distractions and take our time to savor what God is currently showing us about Himself. The gaze upon Christ that leads us to sanctification doesn't thrive when subjected to our demands of time, schedule, and concurrent distractions.

Here's another great example:

> *And we all*, with unveiled faces reflecting the glory
> of the Lord, are being transformed into the same image
> from one degree of glory to another, which is from the
> Lord, who is the Spirit. (2 Corinthians 3:18)

There's beautiful symbolism in that passage—of us as mirrors reflecting the glory of the Lord. When we gaze intently upon Christ, we reflect His nature and glory as it transforms our very person.

A basic mirror requires three characteristics to reflect images well: a light source, a smooth surface, and a material that doesn't absorb photons. In physics, when photons of light strike the surface of an object, the photos are either absorbed, reflected, or scattered. In an ideal mirror, a photon strikes a smooth surface made of reflective material such as polished silver or aluminum. It excites the atoms of the reflective material to such an energized state that the atom must emit energy. The best reflective material emits photons with nearly identical energy as what it received, being extremely responsive to its light source. If there's a smooth surface, the photons emit in a nonrandom manner that accurately reflects the subject. When a photon hits a rough surface (such as choppy water or unpolished metal), light scatters, at best giving a crude reflection of the object. A mirror made of rough material cannot be relied upon for an accurate or well-defined reflection of an image, although there may be somewhat of a reflection. Meanwhile, if the photon strikes material that only absorbs the photon (such as cloth), there's no reflection at all, since the atoms absorb the light but don't get energized and transmit the image by releasing photons.

God is our light source, transmitting the light of the glory of Christ:

> *For God*, who said *"Let light shine out of darkness,"* is the one who shined in our hearts to give us the light of the glorious knowledge of God in the face of Christ. (2 Corinthians 4:6)

He pours His light into us as we read His Word, and His Holy Spirit illuminates our hearts. Of course, like a mirror, we must be turned toward the light source to reflect the light. The more we gaze upon Him through study and worship, the more of His light we're able to respond to.

We're constantly being polished by His Spirit through encouragement, trials, and His Word to rid us of our sinful rough spots so that we can accurately reflect God's exquisite glory. As we receive His light, it excites our inner spirit to the point that we must emit the praise and worship of God's glory to Him and to others. More polishing—and becoming more responsive in our emission of God's glory revealed to us—is the process of sanctification. For some, that process seems to yields primitive spiritual results over an entire lifetime. For others, Christ's glory is clearly seen after a short time.

Why is there this perceived discrepancy among believers, when we have the same Lord and Spirit sanctifying each of us? Should we look at others with spiritual envy and wonder why the Spirit of the Lord seems stronger in them than in us? Why does their degree of sanctification seems greater?

The issues are complex and multifaceted, but one answer often lies in our approach. I've heard people ask these questions, approaching the issue from the premise that they spend just as much time reading the Bible, praying, or serving in the church as more mature Christians do. We must realize that there's no sanctification brought about by completing tasks. Sanctification doesn't result from mere face time with the pages of a Bible or with folded hands, but rather from the presence of our glorious Lord and communion with His Spirit. When the face of Moses began shining, it wasn't because he'd been studying the Ten Commandments to gain some insight or to learn something new. If we approach the Word to gain new knowledge rather than to bask in the worth and worship of Christ, our growth will be stunted. Of course, the Word and prayer are essential for entering into the Lord's presence, but they cannot be the end. That's like the cloth absorbing the light rather than the mirror reflecting it. Those who truly know the Lord spend time in His presence, praising Him for what they know of Him through the Word and the whisperings of the Holy Spirit.

In the physical realm, there's a strong difference between looking and gazing. The eye is controlled by the frontal lobe of the brain when it's "looking" and by the brainstem when it's "gazing." The volitional eye movements (looking) cause the eyes to jump from one target to the next in quick jerky movements called saccades. In gazing, the brainstem allows us to lock our eyes on a target and smoothly follow it nonvolitionally as we completely focus on the object. This is called smooth pursuit. It's impossible to move the eyes smoothly across the field of vision if our eyes aren't fixed in a gaze on a moving target. Try as we might, the eyes bounce from one point to the next in measured intervals. If our eyes are fixed on a target, however, they'll move smoothly along with the target across the field of vision.

This is the difference of spiritual chores versus gazing on Christ. If we approach our time with God to gain something volitionally, our spiritual eyes will bounce here and there, being enamored with a doctrine, a fad, a ministry, a book, a discipline, or a speaker. But when we lock our spiritual eyes on Christ in a gaze, we see Him and follow Him in every area of our lives. We become nonvolitionally enamored with Him. This is the intersection of worship and sanctification.

Gazing upon the Lord is the sanctifying process in all aspects of our walk with God. As Peter learned when he walked on water, we must gaze upon the Lord in the trials of life. As Paul expressed in Philippians 4:12-13, it's through Christ that we're able to endure difficult circumstances. And James tells us that we must pray when we're suffering, and sing praise when we're cheerful (James 5:13).

Gazing upon Christ in all these aspects of the Christian life will rightly turn us to worship Him as we see His sufficiency and supremacy in every occasion of our lives. Although gazing may not necessarily be synonymous with worship, it should always lead to worship.

There's one caveat to gazing upon the Lord. If your desire for worship is to summon cozy feelings about yourself and your faith, you might *not* prefer to gaze entirely upon Him. Similarly, if you only feel good about yourself when you worship, you may be failing to gaze entirely upon Him. True worship doesn't bow to our egocentric desires for warm and fuzzy feelings. These feelings will likely come when we understand the depth of Christ's love for us. But we cannot worship His love without also seeing His holiness and justice. Gazing upon Him requires that we see Him the way His Spirit wants us to see him, not the way we want to see Him.

So may we pray as the psalmist prayed: "Turn my eyes away from what is worthless! Revive me with your Word!" (Psalm 119:137). Let's put on the blinders of Scripture so we don't look to the left or right, but only straight ahead at Christ. As we gaze at Him in awe and worship, the wonderful words of the old hymn will come true in our lives:

> Turn your eyes upon Jesus,
> Look full in His wonderful face,
> And the things of earth will grow strangely dim
> In the light of His glory and grace.

Study Questions

1. What things persuade us to think we don't need more of Christ?

2. Practically, how can you gaze upon Christ at home and at work, in solitude, and in your relationships?

3. Read Colossians 3:9 10. How does worship help us toward inner renewal?

Chapter 6
Worship and Affections

Every individual is a worshiper. We're designed to worship. From the staunchest atheist to the most devout theist, every person on the planet spends his or her life worshiping *something*—one or more things among many. We may or may not be aware that we worship anything, but a check on how we spend our resources is telling. The worship of money may not be purposeful, but many people spend their lives committed to accruing it and its deeper idol of security. The same goes for family, friends, moralism, popularity, power, prestige, success, beauty—so many things can insidiously capture our worship.

It's understandable that this happens to an unbeliever who hasn't experienced God's grace. But why does this also happen to God's people?

We worship that which captures our affections. For example, few people would ever sit down and tell themselves, "Substances that make me feel happy are the most valuable thing in this world, so I'll spend my life worshiping my substance of choice." We tend to worship what makes us happy because those things capture our affections. Of course, when anything besides God promises us long-term happiness, that thing is lying to us.

Of course, God Himself gives us things in this life that are intended to bring pleasure. And while we want to enjoy Him through these pleasurable things He provides for us, our goal is to worship

Him alone as He chiefly captures our affections. If He doesn't capture our affections, we can never will ourselves to truly and consistently worship Him. Any attempt to conjure worship apart from affections will be fruitless and frustrating. Affections and worship are inseparable.

And yet we constantly have affections for things other than God, things that can potentially be the object of our worship. Should we rid our entire lives of everything that could possibly take God's rightful place at the forefront of our affections? If so, we'd probably have to live alone in an empty cave, away from people and every pleasurable object. So how do we ensure that our affections are completely preoccupied with God and His glory?

God helps the Israelites with this dilemma in Deuteronomy 6, where His servant Moses tells them,

> *You must love the LORD your God with your whole mind, your whole being, and all your strength. These words I am commanding you today must be kept in mind, and you must teach them to your children and speak of them as you sit in your house, as you walk along the road, as you lie down, and as you get up. You should tie them as a reminder on your forearm and fasten them as symbols on your forehead. Inscribe them on the doorframes of your houses and gates.* (6:4-9)

Moses then mentions how the Lord is about to bring them into the promised land, "a land with large, fine cities you did not build, houses filled with choice things you did not accumulate, hewn out cisterns you did not dig, and vineyards and olive groves you did not plant" (6:10-11)

And Moses adds this warning:

> *When the LORD your God brings you to the land he promised...and you eat your fill, be careful not to forget the LORD who brought you out of Egypt, that place of slavery. You must revere the LORD your God, serve him, and take oaths using only his name. You must not go after other gods, those of the surrounding peoples, for the LORD your God, who is present among you, is a jealous God and his anger will erupt against you and remove you from the land.* (6:10-15)

God knows that whatever captures the Israelites' love and affection will also capture their worship. And the absolute nonnegotiable is that they worship the one true God of Israel alone. Note that He doesn't demand that the Israelites destroy everything that could replace Him in their affections. He's happy to give them beautiful cities they didn't build, material wealth they didn't accumulate, and bountiful food they didn't grow. His stipulation is that they don't forget the Lord, and that they must worship Him alone. He wants to be at the head of their affections—with every other enjoyable thing acknowledged as a gift from His loving hand.

In specific application to our lives today, we can paraphrase that instruction from Deuteronomy in this way:

> Love the Lord your God with all your being
>
> *by*
>
> keeping God's words in mind, teaching them to your children, and speaking of them as you sit in your house, as you walk along the road, as you lie down, and as you get up

so that

> you will not forget God when you're surrounded by material wealth and foreign gods.

The way to keep God at the fore of our affections is through continuous feeding on His Word. Note that it's through reminders of God's perfect Word, rather than through catchy new insights, that we love and worship Him. The ordinary Israelite of that day knew God's Word, yet they were instructed to keep it ever before their eyes. There was no command to find some new, glamourous interpretation or insight. God's Word as given to us is sufficient for us. That doesn't mean we shouldn't meditate on His Word and ask Him for insight into it. To the contrary, constant rumination on His Word is the vehicle God works through to give us new insight. But we shouldn't rely on gaining new insights to make our walk passionate. Don't cast aside "Sunday school truths" just because you learned them many years ago. They're vital for loving and worshiping God.

Imagine how Christlike we'll become if we focus on Scripture that we keep before our eyes, rather than the latest fashions and entertainments that constantly compete for our attention. The weight of God's glory and kingdom will impress themselves on our heart and draw our affections toward God. The vapidity of all the world's false idols will reveal itself against the light of Scripture that's ever before us.

So read and reread Psalm 23, though you may know it backward and forward. Ask yourself a hundred times a day what it means to love the Lord with your heart, soul, mind, and strength. Dwell on 1 John 4:19, which tells us that we love Him because He first loved us—a beautiful verse that states a theme seen throughout Scripture, to help us desire God in our affections.

When we see God's great desire for us, He truly captures our affections.

Selah

He is the one who sits on the earth's horizon; its inhabitants are like grasshoppers before him.

He is the one who stretches out the sky like a thin curtain, and spreads it out like a pitched tent.

He is the one who reduces rulers to nothing; he makes the earth's leaders insignificant. (Isaiah 40:22-23)

Let the name of God be praised forever and ever, for wisdom and power belong to him.

He changes times and seasons, deposing some kings and establishing others.

He gives wisdom to the wise; he imparts knowledge to those with understanding; he reveals deep and hidden things.

He knows what is in the darkness, and light resides with him. (Daniel 2:20-22)

Jesus Christ is the same yesterday and today and forever! (Hebrews 13:8)

God's Desire for Us

There's a subtle difference between love and desire (using both terms in their pure and nonlustful definitions). A man may love his best friend with true *agape* and *phileo* love. Yet he may go months without talking to that friend, though his heart is truly with him. He may take a bullet for that friend, sit with him through times of grief and trial, or even pass on a romantic interest because of the classic "bro code." But despite his love for that friend, there may not be a daily yearning to be with that person in close fellowship.

Now, consider that same man as he pursues an intimate relationship with the woman he's engaged or married to. His *agape* and *phileo* love for her may be similar to what he shows for his friends and family, but his *desire* for closeness of relationship drives him to continuously pursue a deeper and more active relationship with her. Desire turns up the intensity of a relationship where love already exists.

The root problem in the American church today is not a lack of zeal for God's work. Yes, we sometimes tend toward laziness and complacency, but that's not the heart of the issue. Nor is it a lack of love. We as a group tend to feel love for the Lord. We like to sing songs about Jesus on Sunday morning, spend time in the Word with Him (especially if coffee's involved), and pray to Him from time to time. We generally like most people who like Jesus. And we genuinely love God for His forgiveness and for the future He promises us. But the problem with the American church, at it's heart, is a lack of *desire* for the Lord. Desire to be like Him, and to allow Him, no matter the consequence, to change or remove anything unholy in our lives that comes between us and Him. To say with unqualified resolve, "Here I am, Lord; send me." To devour His Word and bask in the pleasure of communication with Him, worshiping at the foot of His throne in awe and wonder.

Thankfully, we don't have to conjure our own images of what this desire looks like. Long before our hearts turned toward Him, He desired relationship with us. God communed with Adam in the garden of Eden, desiring fellowship with mankind. When we sinned and broke fellowship with God, this set the stage for God to show His desire for us in cosmic magnitude.

Consider His desire for the nation of Israel even in the midst of their unfaithfulness toward God:

> *However, in the future I will allure her; I will lead her back into the wilderness, and speak tenderly to her. From there I*

will give back her vineyards to her, and turn the "Valley of Trouble" into an "Opportunity for Hope."

There she will sing as she did when she was young, when she came up from the land of Egypt.

"At that time," declares the LORD, "you will call, 'My husband'; you will never again call me, 'My master.'

For I will remove the names of the Baal idols from your lips, so that you will never again utter their names!

At that time I will make a covenant for them with the wild animals, the birds of the air, and the creatures that crawl on the ground.

I will abolish the warrior's bow and sword—that is, every weapon of warfare—from the land, and I will allow them to live securely.

I will commit myself to you forever; I will commit myself to you in righteousness and justice, in steadfast love and tender compassion.

I will commit myself to you in faithfulness; then you will acknowledge the LORD." (Hosea 2:14-20)

We learn more of His great desire for His people when His prophet describes the Lord's restoration of fellowship with them:

He takes great delight in you; he renews you by his love; he shouts for joy over you. (Zephaniah 3:17)

Zephaniah depicts this mighty cosmic Warrior being practically giddy over His people. When we see God in light of His omnipotence and sovereignty over the entire universe, His utter control over the galaxies and each microscopic atom, and then we read how passionate He is about His called and chosen ones—how can we refrain from worshiping Him?

And it gets better:

> *And hope does not disappoint, because the love of God has been poured out in our hearts through the Holy Spirit who was given to us. For while we were still helpless, at the right time Christ died for the ungodly. (For rarely will anyone die for a righteous person, though for a good person perhaps someone might possibly dare to die.) But God demonstrates his own love for us, in that while we were still sinners, Christ died for us.* (Romans 5:5-8)

A love that compels God to send His only Son to earth to die for our sins—being pleased even to sacrifice Him in our place (Isaiah 53:10)—demonstrates the hottest desire for us imaginable.

His pursuit of us doesn't stop there, however. He gave us His Holy Spirit as the comforter, guide, and seal of our salvation. He has blessed us with every spiritual blessing in the heavenly places in Christ (Ephesians 1:4). He has lavished His grace upon us (Ephesians 1:6). He chastises us and sends us trials for our growth (Hebrews 12:6), and has given us an eternal inheritance and co-heirship with Christ (1 Peter 1:4; Romans 8:17). The list, of course, goes on and on.

Why does God desire intimacy with us to such a degree? I really don't know. But when I worship and meditate on this aspect of His character, gazing upon His intense desire for us, I find my desire for Him welling up inside me. This desire compels me to be more like Him as I devour His Word, bask in His presence, worship Him in wonder and awe, and allow Him to purge my life from whatever's unholy.

Don't miss this wonderful aspect of your relationship with the Lord. It's one of the most blessed and inexplicable things in the whole

Christian life. When you take the knowledge of God's desire with you through the day, teach it to your children, and give yourself constant reminders of it, it will fan into a roaring fire the spark of our desire for Him. Then, when He's at the center of our affections, we'll truly worship Him as we were meant to. And we'll be able to enjoy all the worldly gifts God gives us without being held hostage by them.

Treasure God

Treasure hunter and diver extraordinaire Mel Fisher lived by one motto: "Today is the day." This treasure-hunting legend had spent his life gaining the skills and knowledge to ensure that someday indeed would be the day of finding his most sought-after treasure. After a few successes that would have satiated the desires of most treasure hunters, Mel turned his attention to seek the find of all finds: the treasure-laden Spanish galleon *Nuestra Senora de Atocha*, sunk in 1622 in a hurricane off of the Florida Keys.

After more than a decade of hard pursuit, he found *Atocha*'s sister ship, *Santa Margarita*, which yielded over twenty million dollars of gold and other treasures. Though it wasn't the *Atocha*, most people would have accepted this finding as life's most generous failings. Not Mel. He searched five more years until he found the *Atocha*, with its forty tons of gold and silver, precious jewels, and other priceless cargo. July 20, 1985, was "the day" — the most significant find since King Tut's tomb in the 1930s.

We must treasure God more than this. Priceless earthly riches do nothing to save souls, bring true joy, or prepare us for eternity. Knowing God does. We must not think of treasuring God the same way that romance novels portray a couple treasuring each other. Romantic treasuring is often portrayed as an enduring love that cherishes the other through trials of life. It's growing old together, and a sweet sort of restful complacency. True treasuring is *seeking*. Desiring. Enduring desperation. Our desire is to know all of God and to worship Him accordingly.

Like Mel Fisher, we shouldn't become complacent with partial discoveries. Satiation with partial discoveries indicates that we treasure God only relatively, maybe valuing Him a bit higher than our possessions or status. But if we live by the exhortation of Scripture, we value God above all else. We must strive to treasure God the Father treasures God the Son, and as God the Son values God the Father—with absolute valuation.

Consider that God the Father has loved and treasured God the Son from eternity past. He shared His glory with Him and they existed in loving communion that surpasses our ability to comprehend. Enter man and sin. God loved us and treasured us absolutely as well. He treasured us to the point that He was willing to crush His treasured Son to redeem Himself to us. In human terms, we might be tempted to say that God the Father treasured us above God the Son, but this is completely untrue. God treasures both us and His Son absolutely. And we must strive to treasure Him and others absolutely as well.

Jesus tells us (in Matthew 6:24) that we cannot serve two masters; we'll love one and hate the other, or else cling to one and despise the other. We cannot serve God and money. From this passage, we see that affections are inextricably connected to worshiping. We serve and worship the one whom we love. Not only that, but this verse precludes our modern church notion of split affections. How many times have we thought, "I can worship God alongside everything else that draws my affections"? But doing that is not within our capability. Once again, the fallacy of relative treasuring tempts us to relatively treasure God above other things we love.

When we treasure God with all our being, worship will come naturally. The pearl of great price will be celebrated. Downturns in the stock market won't dictate the worth of the day. Interpersonal struggles won't determine our level of joy. Only the stench of our sin that hinders us from knowing Him better will horrify us. And we'll boast in the Lord to any ear that will listen.

These are lofty visions, and most of us are far from this point in our journey. To get there, we must say no to the lies that surround us. The lie from the world that only some of God is enough. The lie from the evil one that memorizing God's Word is too difficult, or that speaking of Christ to others is just not for us. The lie from the flesh that our daily routine (sleep included) is more valuable than knowing Christ. The lie from the evil one (similar to the one he used with Eve) that we're incomplete and need something outside of God to complete us. The lie from the world that the riches it offers are all we need. The lie from the flesh that its desires can ever be satiated by filling them.

These are powerful lies that assault us every day, usually many times throughout the day. To fully treasure Christ, along with fully submitting ourselves to His Word and the work of the Holy Spirit, we must continually identify these lies and say no to them.

When we treasure God above all else, we become like the man in Christ's parable who found treasure hidden in a field (Matthew 13:44). Simply for the joy of the treasure, this man sells *all* that he has and buys that field. There's no obligation or reluctance to part with all those possessions. They're gone, and he doesn't give them a second thought because of the joy the newfound treasure brings. If we seek God like this, we'll find Him (Matthew 7:7-8; Proverbs 8:17; Hebrews 11:6). He'll fill our emotional voids with His truth and love. In response, we'll overflow in worship without obligation or reluctance.

When we rejoice in God's Word as one who finds much plunder (Psalm 119:162), we can say with confidence, "Today is the day."

Study Questions

1. Jonathan Edwards wrote that our enjoyment of God "is our proper and...only happiness with which our souls can be satisfied. To go to heaven, fully to enjoy God, is infinitely better than the most pleasant accommodations here. Better than fathers and mothers, husbands, wives, or children, or the company of any or all earthly friends. These are but shadows; but the enjoyment of God is the substance." How do we fully enjoy God here on earth, before we see Him in glory?

2. How does loving God with our heart, soul, mind, and strength relate to desiring God?

3. Write a few sentences about what it would look like for all the people in your church to seek God and desire Him above everything else in their lives.

Chapter 7
In Spirit and in Truth

The first dog I owned was a fun-loving border collie mix named Lucy. Lucy and I went on frequent adventures in the big Texas countryside where I lost myself in imaginative adventure while Lucy bathed herself in cow dung. She also found stock tanks (ponds used to water cattle) and went for muddy swims, which made the stench more complex and full-bodied, adding a fishy smell to the dung. When she found me after her "adventures," she'd be so excited to see me that she tried to rub up against me and give me kisses. But I was never able to get past her fishy dung smell to accept her offerings of adoration.

We've all received gifts that we weren't particularly fond of. Pity the woman whose anniversary gift was a vacuum cleaner, when she wanted jewelry. Or the man who got opera tickets when he wanted tickets for a football game. It's not spite that drives a well-meaning husband to give his wife a vacuum for their anniversary ("It will make vacuuming easier, and it has the latest bells and whistles"), just like it's not malice that drives a woman to get her man opera tickets for a special occasion ("He enjoys spending time with me"). But when we value someone, it's important to ask not only what we want to give, but what that person wants to receive.

On a more significant level, if we view our worship to the Lord as an offering, we must ensure that it's an offering He desires and that we offer it in the way He desires. Concerning worship in general, there are many passages in Scripture where the Lord doesn't accept the sacrifice of worship because the heart is evil. Cain didn't follow God's instructions in worship. Saul disobeyed God in worship. The Israelites didn't bring their best animals for sacrifice. Each of these things caused the Lord to turn away their sacrifices. They might as well have not offered the sacrifice in the first place, because God didn't want it under those circumstances.

Thankfully, we're given guidelines in Scripture for how God wants to be worshiped so that we don't miss the mark. Here are instructions from the Lord Jesus:

> *But a time is coming—and now is here—when the true worshipers will worship the Father in spirit and truth, for the Father seeks such people to be his worshipers. God is spirit, and the people who worship him must worship in spirit and truth."* (John 4:23-24)

He speaks here of "true worshipers." We can infer that there must also be untrue worshipers. Who are those untrue worshipers? Several possibilities exist. They may be those who are mentioned in the previous verses, who attach a specified location to worship (Jerusalem or Samaria). Jesus corrects this error, stating that God will be worshiped regardless of location.

When He says, "A time is coming—and now is here," Jesus is signaling a change in paradigm. The worship of the Old Testament was signified by ceremony, priests, and temples. But now, the believer is to worship anytime in any place. Unfortunately, we slip back into the Old Testament paradigm of temple and ceremony. We tend to offer worship where and when it's offered to us—at our "temple" during our "ceremony" in church. Convenience? Legalism? Although we love to criticize the Old Testament Israelites for their spiritual missteps, we're so much like them. In Jerusalem, in Samaria, in the temple, in the church, and in the presence of a band are not the only places where worship should be offered. Quite to the contrary, God desires worship from all walks of life in all locations. There's no special place where His Spirit more readily descends on us to suddenly transform us into worshipers. Worship is much more dependent on the Spirit *in* us than the Spirit *on* us.

Another possibility is that the "true worshipers" refers to all believers. All who have been redeemed by the blood of Christ are expected to be worshipers of God. Not only expected to be worshipers, but *sought out* to be worshipers. This means that God wants you and me to have our own robes and folders in His everyday choir. It means that our worship of God identifies us as Christians, and is one of the gauges of maturity in our walk with God. This is quite a calling to live up to. Although our salvation is apart from works, God sought us and saved us to be worshipers of Him.

The true worshipers in the passage could also be referring to the subset of Christians who commit to worshiping God in spirit and in truth. This would be in contrast to Christians who are lazy in worship and hardly ever offer it, or those who worship in untruth. The passage repeats the importance of worshiping in spirit and in truth for emphasis and states that true worshipers *must* worship in spirit and in truth.

If we honestly examine our own lives of worship, we may find that we fall into routines of public or corporate worship that are both unspirited and truth-lacking. So let's examine what it means to worship in spirit and in truth so that we can be those whom God is seeking to worship Him.

In Spirit

The Greek word used for "spirit" in John 4:23-24 is *pneumati*. Some form of this word is used in the New Testament for Holy Spirit (Luke 3:16; Mark 12:36), for the nonphysical part of the being (Matthew 5:3; Mark 2:8), for individuals in the Spirit world (Mark 5:2; Luke 8:29), and for characteristics or attitudes of an individual (Romans 12:11; 1 Corinthians 4:21; Galatians 6:1). There's no specification of which of these is meant when we're told to worship in spirit, but several of them certainly apply.

Without the Holy Spirit of God, our worship is meaningless. His illumination enables our spirit to understand the things of God. Without this illumination, our prayers and song lyrics are only words. We cannot worship what hasn't been supernaturally revealed to us, or else we engage in false worship. The Israelites fell into this literal deathtrap.

In Exodus 32, we're given the account of the forging of the golden calf. Moses had gone up onto Mount Sinai to receive the tablets of testimony written by the finger of God. When he was delayed in coming down, the people grew spiritually restless. They demanded physical gods to go before them (32:1) because they didn't know what had become of Moses, their spiritual leader. Nowhere in the passage does it explicitly state that they knowingly and willfully rejected the God of Abraham, Isaac, and Jacob. However, they were so spiritually dull that they attributed their exodus from Egypt to the man Moses (32:1), and they worshiped the calf as "the gods who brought [them] out of Egypt" (32:4,8). What dim spiritual eyes! Aaron even declared a feast to the Lord Yahweh on the following day.

Their sin wasn't lack of worship, nor was it conscious and willful devil worship. Their sin was the lack of spiritual sight. They couldn't see their Bridegroom's glory, and this turned them toward spiritual prostitution. God takes our worship of Him seriously, and because they failed to worship Him according to how He'd revealed Himself to them, their dullness that day cost them their lives.

Our worship apart from the Holy Spirit is no different. Like the Israelites worshiping "the gods that brought them out of Egypt," we sometimes worship what gives us peace, prosperity, and that which makes us feel good about ourselves. Even some of our worship songs are filled with glorifying who *we* are (in Christ, of course) and the fact that we're strong enough to get through the trials of life (in Christ, of course). We must make sure that we're sensitive to the teaching and illumination of the Holy Spirit, and that the Holy Spirit fully guides our worship. Paul emphasizes in Philippians 3:3 that the mark of the spiritually circumcised is worshiping by the Spirit of God. Let's not make the same disastrous mistake that the Israelites made.

Worshiping in spirit can also refer to the attitude or characteristic of our worship. As a former Sunday morning worship leader, I've seen the most bored and lifeless faces when looking out into the congregation. Of course, there are also people who are truly spirited in their worship. I think our private worship lives are no different; some are dull and boring, others full of spirit. We, of course, want to be those who offer worship in a spirited attitude. But not all spirited offerings of worship are pleasing to the Lord, as Nadab and Abihu taught us in Leviticus 10:1-3.

What is the spirit in which God wants us to worship? In 2 Samuel 6, we're given the account of David dancing before the Lord. Three characteristics of the spirit of true worship stand out from this passage: joy (verse 12), fervor (14) and humility (21-22).

When a friend greets you without a smile and seems otherwise unengaged, that friendship is probably unlikely to last. If they're browsing on their electronic devices the entire time they're with you, it's reasonable to assume they're merely tolerant of your presence. But it's the joy in a relationship that makes that relationship meaningful. So how can we possibly approach without joy the worship of our Master who has given us everything?

Psalm 98:4 tells us, "Shout out praises to the LORD, all the earth! Break out in a joyful shout and sing!" The spirit of joy is not only essential for worship that God desires, it's also truly pleasant for us, as we saw earlier. If joy is missing in your life of worship, examine why it isn't there. Maybe we forget what we've been saved from, or the kind of family into which we've been adopted. Maybe we fail to realize the gloriousness and accessibility of God. Maybe the trinkets of this world are more valuable to us than Christ. There's no excuse for just being a sourpuss—no sourpuss ever saved from the pits of hell by God's grace is meant to remain a sourpuss. So start showing the joy of being in the presence of our great and glorious Master!

When an individual is described as "spirited," we often think of fervor and energy. Fervor is certainly a necessary component for quality worship. Contemplate the definition that Webster's 1828 dictionary gives for *fervor*: heat of mind; ardor; warm or animated zeal and earnestness in the duties of religion, particularly in prayer. Imagine a thermometer in your mind when you worship. Is the temperature rising as you engage in spirited worship? It's the heat of mind and animated zeal that David displayed when he celebrated energetically (2 Sam 6:5) and danced with all his strength (2 Samuel 6:14) before the Lord. Our worship should be equally engaged.

Just as you shouldn't be stuck in apathy—fervor's opposite— make sure you don't settle for fervor's counterfeit, which is emotionalism. Physical displays of worship and impassioned tears during worship don't necessarily signal a heat of mind, although they may. Getting caught up in the emotion of a concert is a wonderful thing and might sometimes lead us to true worship. Even if we're not truly worshiping, a good concert does good for the soul. But we shouldn't settle for the welling up of the soul to replace our spiritual worship of God.

Here's the check: If you find the same impassioned body language being used in your daily time of worship, you're likely in David's camp of fervor. If this body language is used only when other people are around or when loud and emotional music is playing, you might be settling for the counterfeit of emotionalism.

A. W. Tozer's observation from the last century still applies:

> Much of the singing in certain types of meetings has in
> it more of romance than it has of the Holy Ghost. Both
> words and music are designed to rouse the libidinous.
> Christ is courted with a familiarity that reveals a total
> ignorance of who He is. It is not the reverent intimacy
> of the adoring saint but the impudent familiarity of the
> carnal lover.

God intends to rule in our spirits Himself, and for our spirits to control our mind, and for our minds to control our flesh and emotions. When this chain of command works correctly, God guides our spirits through His Spirit and His Word. Our spirit then instructs our mind how to think. Our mind, controlled by the Spirit and steeped in Scripture, then controls the urges of the flesh and guides our emotions to be honoring to God and constructive to ourselves. In this way, our emotions, bodies, and minds can all be pleasing to the Lord.

It's unhealthy, however, when this chain of command is backward. When our emotions or flesh dominate our minds, we're sickly Christians, prone to wandering and backsliding. The warnings of Romans 6:13 come to fruition. We're a ship on stormy seas without a rudder. While in today's Christianity we're well aware of the dangers of living according to the flesh, we're less wary of living according to our emotions. This isn't a danger to be dismissed, because we're not strong enough to merely ignore our emotions. They, like the flesh, can deceive, entice, and ambush our spiritual well-being if not kept in check. Emotions themselves are not evil, just as the body itself is not evil. But when unchecked, emotions strive to control the mind and spirit. We should rather steep the mind in Scripture and the control of the Holy Spirit so that it can control the emotions and the flesh. In so doing, we won't succumb to the counterfeit of emotionalism.

We also must ensure that we don't allow the mind to control the emotions and flesh independently of the Spirit. The mind apart from the Spirit will control the emotions by using worldly means that can wreck our spiritual lives, such as positive thinking, inordinate self-care, and materialism. We must restore the complete chain of command: Scripture-filled spirit over mind, and mind over emotions and flesh.

The antithesis to fervor is apathy, and this is what develops when our mind controls our spirit. Our walk with the Lord is dry. We develop an agenda for how we want our spiritual growth to occur. After we attempt to manhandle our own walk with the Lord, we become critical of others' walk with the Lord because they don't share our agenda. A pattern of criticizing others, especially those who are godly, is a sure sign that our mind is dominating our spirit, instead of the other way around. This will annihilate fervor of worshiping in spirit.

We've already touched on the importance of the spirit of humility in worship. When David danced before the Lord, he was criticized by his wife Michal for the shame and humiliation he brought on himself by his display. David's response is something we do well to remember: "It was before the Lord! I was celebrating before the Lord... I am willing to shame and humiliate myself even more than this!" (2 Samuel 6:21-22). Our expression of worship should be for the Lord only, and we should be willing to shame and humiliate ourselves limitlessly to sing His praises. This includes our conversations with unbelievers who may be hostile to the faith. It includes when we're around Christians who might think we're weird for worshiping outside of church. It also includes when we're in church, if the Lord leads us to belt out His praises among those who are merely mouthing words of the song. We worship for the Lord alone.

After David dances and worships before the Lord, he leads the congregation vocally in worship, as we see in 1 Chronicles 16. It's a beautiful mix of his own worship and a call to spirited worship. His desire is that all may know the blessings of true worship. It's the way he came before the Lord's presence, and we would be wise to do the same.

Meditate on these verses from David's song, and apply them in your worship life; they have everything we need to learn how to offer truly spirited worship:

Give thanks to the Lord! Call on his name! Make known his accomplishments among the nations!

Sing to him! Make music to him!

Tell about all his miraculous deeds! Boast about his holy name! Let the hearts of those who seek the LORD rejoice!

Seek the LORD and the strength he gives! Seek his presence continually!

Recall the miraculous deeds he performed, his mighty acts and the judgments he decreed.
(1 Chronicles 16:8-12)

Sing to the LORD, all the earth! Announce every day how he delivers!

Tell the nations about his splendor, tell all the nations about his miraculous deeds!

For the LORD is great and certainly worthy of praise, he is more awesome than all gods.

For all the gods of the nations are worthless, but the LORD made the heavens.

Majestic splendor emanates from him, he is the source of strength and joy.

Ascribe to the LORD, O families of the nations, ascribe to the LORD splendor and strength!

Ascribe to the LORD the splendor he deserves!

Bring an offering and enter his presence!

Worship the LORD in holy attire!

Tremble before him, all the earth! The world is established, it cannot be moved. Let the heavens rejoice, and the earth be happy! Let the nations say, "The LORD reigns!"

Let the sea and everything in it shout! Let the fields and everything in them celebrate! Then let the trees of the forest shout with joy before the Lord, for he comes to judge the earth!

*Give thanks to the L*ORD*, for he is good and his loyal love endures.*

Say this prayer: "Deliver us, O God who delivers us! Gather us! Rescue us from the nations! Then we will give thanks to your holy name, and boast about your praiseworthy deeds."

*May the L*ORD *God of Israel be praised, in the future and forevermore.* (1 Chronicles 16:23-36)

Selah

From east to west the LORD's name is deserving of praise.

The LORD is exalted over all the nations; his splendor reaches beyond the sky.

Who can compare to the LORD our God, who sits on a high throne?

He bends down to look at the sky and the earth.

He raises the poor from the dirt, and lifts up the needy from the garbage pile, that he might seat him with princes, with the princes of his people.

He makes the barren woman of the family a happy mother of children.

Praise the LORD! (Psalm 113:3-9)

Oh, the depth of the riches and wisdom and knowledge of God! How unsearchable are his judgments and how fathomless his ways! For who has known the mind of the Lord, or who has been his counselor? Or who has first given to God, that God needs to repay him? For from him and through him and to him are all things. To him be glory forever! Amen. (Romans 11:33-36)

In Truth

We all have friends or family members who think they know us much better than they do. They make confident statements to you and others about what your character and personality is like. The statement usually starts, "The thing about you is..." or, "You've always been one to..." Especially when people misfire on their rash assumptions about me, I find myself wondering why they don't just ask me about myself. Sometimes it's so bad, I think they don't even know me. When people do that with me, it's annoying; when we do it with God, it's disastrous.

In Ezekiel 13, God strongly condemns Israel's false prophets for saying they speak in God's name while really using only their own imaginations (13:2). It seems that these prophets weren't rejecting God outright, as Jonah did, but rather were being careless with God's character and treating the heavy things of God lightly. They're described as foolish and as following their own spirit (13:3). They were under delusion. God says they were like jackals among ruins, implying that they were scavenging for recognition. Interestingly, the passage also states that the prophets thought their own words would come true (13:6). Their error didn't seem to be that of knowledgeably twisting God's words; it was rather that they spoke authoritatively without first seeking out God's own message. Some of the lies they spoke are still widely in circulation today: promising peace and prosperity despite the nation's rebellion, minimizing sin, and covering up evil.

God is zealous for His truth, and He doesn't take our ignorance lightly. Whether it's His message or His character, we must carefully study theology so we don't speak as those prophets did in Ezekiel 13. Being nice and loving Jesus doesn't give us a free pass to mischaracterize our great God. No Christian should ever slight the deep things of God by saying things like, "Doctrine divides, so avoid it for the sake of unity," or "Theologians have debated this topic for millennia, so it's not important to take a stance." When we get to heaven, we'll likely find out that we were wrong on some of the more challenging points of doctrine. But in our journey here on earth, we love the Lord with our whole mind by striving to know Him better—to better understand every single facet of His revealed character in the Word.

To worship Him, we must know Him. We don't know Him when we tell others it's okay to live in sexual immorality, because God just wants you to be happy. Nor do we know Him when we excuse a quick temper because "that's just how he is," or "she's a work in progress." Furthermore, when we sing our songs of praise to God, we must ensure that the God they describe matches the God in the Bible. Not all songs that get published are accurate.

Our knowledge of truth should be deep as well as accurate. I remember when Katherine and I first started getting to know each other. We played a game called Would You Rather in which we took turns describing scenarios, and the other person had to state which scenario he or she would choose. "Would you rather have a house infested by cockroaches or by ants? Would you rather be forced to eat tacos every meal for the rest of your life, or never eat tacos again?" Although this game is fun in the early stages of a friendship or romantic relationship, I'm glad Katherine and I moved beyond it and have grown to know each other more deeply. Our deeper knowledge of each other has come from intentional conversations and from sharing life's experiences with each other. It's the normal way for a marriage relationship to proceed. If we'd never moved on from getting-to-know-you games to deeper conversations and shared life experiences, we wouldn't have much of a marriage.

Our relationship with God is similar. If we merely coast on what we learned about God in our early walk, we miss out on the deep and beautiful romance we can have with Him. As our knowledge of Him deepens, so should our worship of Him. The truth of His character is so much more than just His love for us, so our worship should be more than just repeating "He loves me" twenty times.

In Job's encounter with his friends, Job is asked these questions: "Can you discover the depths of God? Can you discover the limits of the Almighty?… Do you hear the secret counsel of God, and limit wisdom to yourself?" (Job 11:7; 15:8 NASB). Of course, the rhetorical answer is no, but that should encourage us to press on even harder in our quest to know God more deeply. After all, Christ and His Word are the very truth (John 14:6; 17:17). When we know God's doctrines intimately, we'll then be able to worship Him in truth.

To worship the Lord in spirit and in truth certainly encompasses more than worshiping according to the Holy Spirit, worshiping in joy, fervor, and humility, and worshiping with accurate and deep doctrine. This is, however, a great start. In our prayers, the spirit will ensure that our worship is more than a doctrinal exercise, and our mind will ensure that we aren't seeking emotional gratification. Let's follow Paul's example in 1 Corinthians 14:15: " I will sing praises with my spirit, but I will also sing praises with my mind." This is the worship and worshiper that God seeks.

Study Questions

1. How can spirit and truth complement each other in worship? How can they antagonize each other?

2. Read Matthew 6:7. What are we warned against? Why is it bad? What are some ways that we do this?

3. Read Acts 18:24-28. From this passage, list some characteristics of a fervent individual.

Chapter 8
Through the Storm

The storms of life will come. They cannot be avoided, and we shouldn't try to avoid them. It's helpful to think of the storms in life for what they really are—mere loss or fear of loss. It may be financial loss, loss of loved ones, loss of dignity, loss of life, loss of love or respect, or loss of anything else we value. For the believer, loss is an opportunity to gain Christ. When we love and value earthly things (even good things that the Lord may have given us), we risk idolatry—setting something up as equal to or above God in our affections. When we lose these things of value to us, it gives us the opportunity to reconstitute our valuation of Christ above all else.

Although any loss is difficult—even if what's lost was never an idol for us—the worship of God fills the void to overflowing, because in worship we remind our souls that God is more valuable than anything in this life. Therefore, in worship we don't need to fear loss in the storms of life, because we know who our true treasure is.

We shouldn't expend excessive energy to avoid loss. Individuals who don't know Christ (as well as many who do) spend their entire lives and assets trying to avoid the storms or trials of life. Around their "kingdoms" they build impenetrable walls that they think will help them avoid loss. In the center of these man-made kingdoms is an idol that promises to give them the two most coveted things in this life—peace and joy.

For instance, when one fears financial loss and insecurity, he works fiendishly to build his bank account. He may sacrifice time with God, time building up the church body, and even time with his family (after all, he's trying to shelter them from financial hardship) so he can avoid this storm. He doesn't give money back to the Lord, or does so only insignificantly. Money becomes his idol, and he'll do anything to keep from losing it. Unfortunately, he finds that more money doesn't bring him peace and joy; it brings only an increased desire for even more money to insulate him and his loved ones from financial hardship.

Or think of the mother who deeply loves her family. She may begin to fear the day when she loses her family—perhaps physical loss of her husband or spiritual loss of her children to the vices of the world. In an effort to prevent this loss, she may build her kingdom with strong and impenetrable walls of frequent designated family time. She becomes domineering in teaching her children and often critical of others in an attempt to keep her family close to her. She controls her family and won't let them out of her sight. Family has become her idol, and she'll do anything to guard that idol from loss.

There's no peace or joy in idol worship. Ironically, the very joy and peace we look for in our kingdoms and idols will be ours only when we tear down those kingdoms and idols and worship the one true God.

Take a moment to examine your life. We're all guilty of building some kingdom and worshiping some idol apart from (or in addition to) God, in our effort to find more peace and joy.

Because kingdom-building always starts with fear of loss of the idol, worshiping God in His rightful place on the throne of your life can help you quell the fear, snuff out the idolatry, and regain joy and peace in life as you lay aside the exhausting work of protecting your kingdom and idol. It frees you to build God's kingdom and build up others in the faith, since you no longer feel compelled to frantically build your idol's kingdom.

Worship constantly places our affections on things above, not on things of the earth. In doing so, it turns the loss of things we value into the gain of Christ. The storms of loss still come, but instead of being destroyed by a kingdom collapsing on our heads, we're strengthened spiritually by turning to the Lord in worship.

But sometimes things feel different when we're actually inside the storm.

Worshiping from Inside the Storm

We need to train our spirits to recognize trials as a trigger for worship. The wind and the waves rock us. Our footing seems unsure. The driving rain stings our eyes and blurs our vision of reality. We're cold and wet, chilled to the bone. Our head is exploding with anguish from within and imploding from the grinding trials without.

Our natural response is to question God's goodness and sovereignty. I find myself praying, "Lord, I've always served You; don't abandon me!" Funny how I don't question God's sovereignty or goodness when all seems right with the world.

Trials are the times when faith and worship come together and have their finest hour. They're the moment we prepare for during our prayer and study of the Word. They're the battle for which we sharpen our spiritual swords with the study and memory of Scripture, with the learning of hymns and praise songs, and with the building of a robust prayer life. A sharp sword is no help if it isn't used in battle. So we fight in the storm through the power of the Holy Spirit who uses all those things to keep us walking closely with God, eyes confidently fixed on Him to produce joy and peace through it all.

In 2 Chronicles 20, Judah's King Jehoshaphat was faced with a mighty storm. Three armies had assembled into a "huge army" (20:2) to fight against Israel. Jehoshaphat's response was a natural one: fear (20:3). However, he didn't wallow in this fear and allow it to drive him to act as an unbeliever. Certainly, even as believers, we would probably not fault him for immediately consulting his military strategists or calling the people to arms. We might even think it reasonable for him to call out an S-O-S prayer to petition rescue.

The prayer he actually offered is remarkable:

> *O LORD God of our ancestors, you are the God who lives in heaven and rules over all the kingdoms of the nations. You possess strength and power; no one can stand against you. Our God, you drove out the inhabitants of this land before your people Israel and gave it as a permanent possession to the descendants of your friend Abraham. They settled down in it and built in it a temple to honor you, saying, "If disaster comes on us in the form of military attack, judgment, plague, or famine, we'll stand in front of this temple before you, for you are present in this temple. We will cry out to you for help in our distress, so that you will hear and deliver us."*
> (2 Chronicles 20:6-9)

Among the people hearing this prayer, I wonder how many were thinking, "We're about to get obliterated—and our king is worshiping God?" Interestingly, the worshipful part of Jehoshaphat's prayer is longer than the supplication part, which follows in verses 10-12.

Then, through a prophet, the Lord answered Jehoshaphat's prayers (20:13-18), giving assurance of victory. Can you guess how this godly man responded?

> *Jehoshaphat bowed down with his face toward the ground, and all the people of Judah and the residents of Jerusalem fell down before the LORD and worshiped him. Then some Levites, from the Kohathites and Korahites, got up and loudly praised the LORD God of Israel.* (20:18-19)

The next day, right before battle, Jehoshaphat addressed the people again:

> *Jehoshaphat stood up and said: "Listen to me, you people of Judah and residents of Jerusalem! Trust in the LORD your God and you will be safe! Trust in the message of his prophets and you will win." He met with the people and appointed musicians to play before the LORD and praise his majestic splendor. As they marched ahead of the warriors they said: "Give thanks to the LORD, for his loyal love endures." When they began to shout and praise, the LORD suddenly attacked the Ammonites, Moabites, and men from Mount Seir who were invading Judah, and they were defeated. (20:20-22)*

The combination of faith and worship is itself our victory against the storm. God may or may not intervene to remove our circumstances, as He did with Jehoshaphat. It doesn't really matter. The reward for blind faith and worship despite circumstances is joy and peace through anything that life can throw at us, rather than removal of circumstances. When God looks down from heaven on a child of His who blindly trusts Him and adores Him with praise no matter what, He must be proudly saying, "That's my child. Well done."

This of course doesn't mean that in the storm we'll always want to worship or feel like worshiping. Those who say worshiping always involves happy emotion have never been through a worthy storm. Sometimes during a storm we're able to say, "All things work together for good to those who love God and are called according to His purpose." But there are times when the storm gets so intense, and beats us down with such ferocity, that we can only blindly hold on to this dear truth: "The Lord gives and the Lord takes away. Blessed be the name of the Lord." This too is worship—whether our happiness is bubbling over or nonexistent. Irrespective of our feelings, the worship of God's attributes is the anchor that keeps us from capsizing during the storm.

Selah

Do you know the laws of the heavens, or can you set up their rule over the earth?

Can you raise your voice to the clouds so that a flood of water covers you?

Can you send out lightning bolts, and they go? Will they say to you, 'Here we are'?

Who has put wisdom in the heart, or has imparted understanding to the mind? (Job 38:33-36)

I am the LORD! That is my name!

I will not share my glory with anyone else, or the praise due me with idols.

Look, my earlier predictive oracles have come to pass; now I announce new events.

Before they begin to occur, I reveal them to you."

Sing to the LORD a brand new song!

Praise him from the horizon of the earth, you who go down to the sea, and everything that lives in it, you coastlands and those who live there! (Isaiah 42:8-10)

What to Do with a Bad Day

How often we need this anchor of worship! We often have "bad days" when we feel in the very core of our being that everything has gone wrong. Perhaps we've made a mess of a relationship and now have an unshakeable fear of losing that person. Perhaps we've done everything right at work and things still seem nauseatingly out of control and against our favor. Usually it's a combination and build-up of many things that cause *weltschmerz*—the weariness of this world.

Unfortunately, our list of problems will only lengthen if we react poorly by speaking harshly to others (usually those we love) or by withdrawing from those who can help us. We find ourselves in the bottom of a valley, wistfully longing for the upswing of our fortunes and a chance to get ourselves back in control of life. If we turn to God, we often see the waves crashing around us and look to the Lord out of fear and desperation, grasping for His hand.

What is a bad day, but failing to realize the working of God's plan in the events surrounding our lives? Once we realize that all things work for His glory and kingdom, the pain, anxiety, and brokenness turn into joy. We see the waves and the wind as objects of His creation, meant to bring Him glory. They're powerful, but He is so much more powerful.

We see His love in the trial and remember His faithfulness to us. Then, as the waves are crashing around us, we look to the Lord not from fear but from confidence. The reorientation that results from worship allows us to see the greatness of God and His plan for us in His universe. One glimpse of this, and we relinquish the tight grasp of control that drives us to agony.

The disciples learned this when they took a boat ride with the Jesus, as we see in Matthew 8. When the storms drove them to the brink of anxiety, they called upon the Lord to save them. Aren't we supposed to go to Jesus with our problems? Why then did Jesus rebuke them? It's because they called to Him from fear rather than confidence.

After Jesus calmed the storm, they spoke in awe and reverence: "What kind of man is this? Even the wind and sea obey Him!"—a confession of God's omnipotence. If they'd started with this confession of worship, they would have found themselves waking Jesus in the boat only after making bets with each other on how He would save them from the storm.

Our bad days go so much better if we race our worship of the Lord against His intervening actions, and our worship wins. Too often we wait to see God show up for us in a situation before we'll worship Him. If our worship of Him precedes His actions, then He absolutely will show up for us. He may not calm the storm around us, but through our worship He'll calm the storm inside us. As we focus on His love and power, the words "Peace, be still" will resonate in our hearts, and we'll have what the entire world is looking for— peace and joy in the storms of life.

This allows us to take our clutching, grasping hands off the steering wheel of our life. We then grow deeper in our knowledge and trust of Him, and we move to the passenger seat, letting God drive, even though we may still be telling Him where we want to go in life.

Then, as yet more faith comes through the worship of His character, we move to the back seat, where we rest in His driving and navigating, though we may frequently ask, "Where are we going?" and "Are we there yet?"

Finally, the fruit of joy and peace are set when we trust him fully and relocate to the outside bed of the truck of life, where we have only to enjoy the ride and the views and the wind in our hair. We fully trust the driver to get us where we're going safely. Otherwise, we're clutching the steering wheel of life, careening down the highway blindfolded and anxious.

Let's give the steering wheel of our life to the One who's sovereign over all, while we sit back and enjoy the ride.

Study Questions

1. How do we know when we're building our own kingdom instead of God's kingdom?

2. Is it invariably true that trials always bring us closer to God?

3. How can we avoid the collapse of our spirits when we lose things we love?

4. What's the relationship between trust and peace?

5. Compare the account of Job to that of Lot's wife (Genesis 19:26). How could Lot's wife have avoided true loss in the storm?

Chapter 9
Sketches of Worshippers

You can tell a lot about a person's theology and spiritual health by the object and nature of their worship. You can tell a lot about a person's object and nature of worship by the schedule they keep and the subjects of their conversations. If someone worships leisure, you can bet that an examination of his worship life will show a schedule filled with entertainment, social gatherings, or other such leisure activities. If a believer worships knowledge, you may hear dry diatribes about doctrine and dismay at the modern church's lack of doctrinal accuracy. If someone worships affirmation, you may hear about how doctrine isn't important, and how love is the only thing that matters.

But a believer who understands the revealed character of the God from the Bible, and who walks closely with Him, will have prayers and conversations filled with awe inspired by God's attributes. This is something Jesus clearly teaches:

> The good person out of the good treasury of his heart produces good, and the evil person out of his evil treasury produces evil, for his mouth speaks from what fills his heart. (Luke 6:45)

As in the modern church, the Bible is filled both with individuals who grasped God's greatness in their hearts and with those who did not. For our benefit, their words, prayers, and thoughts are recorded, reflecting the contents of their hearts. Let's briefly examine some of them to see what aspects of worship we can implement in our own lives.

Nebuchadnezzar—the Bad, the Ugly, and the Good

There are few characters in Scripture whose worship lives are so easy to relate to as King Nebuchadnezzar. We may not be able to relate to his position as a powerful king, or even to his spiritual position, since we don't know for sure whether he trusted in God's redemptive plan for mankind. However, his worship patterns and tendencies elicit the same roars of dismay and huzzahs of affirmation that can be found when I examine my own life of worship.

Our first encounter of Nebuchadnezzar's worship of God is found in Daniel 2, after Daniel has accurately described the king's dream and interpreted the meaning of it.

> *Then King Nebuchadnezzar bowed down with his face to the ground and paid homage to Daniel. He gave orders to offer sacrifice and incense to him. The king replied to Daniel, "Certainly your God is a God of gods and Lord of kings and revealer of mysteries, for you were able to reveal this mystery!"* (Daniel 2:46-47)

Note that Nebuchadnezzar actually falls on his face and does homage to Daniel! This sounds like *proskyneo*—but to a man instead of to God. However, Nebuchadnezzar then proceeds to magnify the Lord, presumably in front of the entire court, by saying that God is above all gods and kings. The king seems unsure whether to worship Daniel or God, so he does both.

Nebuchadnezzar's problem was that he allowed divine interaction to come solely through a godly man, instead of seeking the Lord himself. How often we do the same thing! We don't seek the Lord as ardently as we should. Instead we're content to be fed inspiration and worship from other people who are seeking the Lord.

As A. W Tozer said in *The Pursuit of God*, "How tragic that we in this dark day have had our seeking done for us by our teachers."

This is a common attitude in worship as well. Do we wait for songs, bands, and worship leaders to bring us into God's presence? Unfortunately, this easily leads to adoration of the band that was necessary to lead us into worship. We may identify our spiritual selves by styles of music, teachers, and authors, as the early Corinthian church erroneously did (1 Corinthians 3:4-7), rather than seeking for ourselves the worship and wisdom from the Holy Spirit above all treasure. This deprives us of the blessing of seeking the Lord with our whole hearts, communing with Him daily, and yearning to be taught of Him. As we rely on others for our spiritual well-being, we elevate them to a place where God and God alone should be. He alone is the vine, and we're the branches; we get our spiritual life from abiding in Him.

Like many of us, Nebuchadnezzar had a short attention span. In Daniel 3, we see him making a large idol and proclaiming that every subject in his kingdom must worship it under threat of death. I don't think his idolatry was directed toward make-believe gods, but rather toward his own perceived greatness. We know from other passages that he's quite the narcissist. Eleven times in Daniel 3, it's specifically mentioned that this was the image Nebuchadnezzar had made or set up. This redundancy is not accidental, but reminds us of all the warnings from God to not worship the works of our hands—which is really a form of self-worship (Isaiah 2:8; Jeremiah 1:16).

Nebuchadnezzar was worshiping the work of his hands, and as king he had the power to force others to bow before it. Don't we often do the same? We sometimes err by valuing above all else the little kingdoms we build with our hands—career, family, ministry, financial security, and reputation. We fight with all our strength to protect these little kingdoms, and we become quite agitated when they seem threatened. Instead, we should worship God and seek to add only to His kingdom.

When Nebuchadnezzar's idol of power was threatened by

Shadrach, Meshach, and Abednego (Daniel's godly friends), the king lashed out with rage. This is a natural response when our idols are threatened. But God delivered those three men from the king's wrath, a deliverance which prompted Nebuchadnezzar to again worship God.

Note however that the king's worship in both chapters 2 and 3 is quite impersonal. He refers to God as the God of Daniel, or as the God of Shadrach, Meshach, and Abednego. Also, Nebuchadnezzar's praise revolves only around what God has done in those circumstances, and not around who God is. It would seem that Nebuchadnezzar viewed himself as an impressed competitor with God.

The next chapter in Daniel begins with Nebuchadnezzar declaring "to all peoples, nations, and language groups" the signs and wonders that God has done for him (Daniel 4:1-3). He's using worship as a means to further God's kingdom. We can do that too! To introduce people to our God by vocally worshiping who He is and what He has done for us, we don't need extensive training, intricate programs, or advanced degrees (although all can potentially be good things).

After expressing this praise for God, Nebuchadnezzar then recounts (in 4:4-33) what's behind it: his amazing personal story of how God had humbled him by driving him into the wilderness as an animal. Prior to that experience, Nebuchadnezzar had worshiped his own greatness (4:30), but through this humiliating ordeal, he finally finds true worship:

> *At the end of the appointed time I, Nebuchadnezzar, looked up toward heaven, and my sanity returned to me. I extolled the Most High, and I praised and glorified the one who lives forever. For his authority is an everlasting authority, and his kingdom extends from one generation to the next. All the inhabitants of the earth are regarded as nothing.*
>
> *He does as he wishes with the army of heaven and with those who inhabit the earth. No one slaps his hand and says to him, "What have you done?"* (4:34-35)

Moses

In Exodus 15, the song of praise from the heart of Moses is so much more than mere thanksgiving to God for what He'd done for the Israelites. Pragmatically, Moses might have simply uttered under his breath, "Thank You, Lord, for delivering us." But Moses deems it more fitting to honor God with extravagant love and extreme submission, focusing more on who God is than on what He'd done for the Israelites. He thanks God for what He did for them, but this is only a small portion of his song of praise.

Let's look at some of the ways that his song worships and magnifies God for who He is, in addition to what He did for them:

The LORD is my strength and song,
And He has become my salvation;
This is my God, and I will praise Him;
My father's God, and I will exalt Him.
The LORD is a warrior;
The LORD is His name. (15:2)

Your right hand, O LORD, was majestic in power,
Your right hand, O LORD, shattered the enemy.
In the abundance of your majesty You overthrow
those who rise up against You;
You sent forth Your wrath;
it consumed them like stubble. (15:6-7)

Who is like You, O LORD, among the gods?
Who is like You, majestic in holiness,
Fearful in praises, working wonders? (15:11)

The LORD will reign forever and ever! (15:18)

A few chapters later in Exodus, we read about Moses encountering Jethro, his father-in-law, whom he hadn't seen for some time. As they asked about each other's welfare, Moses didn't complain to Jethro about how the grumbling Israelites were making his life so difficult. This is especially impressive since in the previous chapter, we read how Moses had feared for his life when the people grumbled about not having food, meat, and water.

Moses also took no credit for the great things that had happened to Israel. He related the story of God's goodness to the people in a way that caused Jethro to realize that God is greater than all gods. The result was that Jethro also praised God, rejoicing in His goodness and worshiping His greatness. Here's the passage:

> *Moses told his father-in-law all that the LORD had done to Pharaoh and to Egypt for Israel's sake, and all the hardship that had come on them along the way, and how the LORD had delivered them. Jethro rejoiced because of all the good that the LORD had done for Israel, whom he had delivered from the hand of Egypt. Jethro said, "Blessed be the LORD who has delivered you from the hand of Egypt, and from the hand of Pharaoh, who has delivered the people from the Egyptians' control! Now I know that the LORD is greater than all the gods, for in the thing in which they dealt proudly against them he has destroyed them." Then Jethro, Moses' father-in-law, brought a burnt offering and sacrifices for God, and Aaron and all the elders of Israel came to eat food with the father-in-law of Moses before God. (Exodus 18:8-12)*

What a powerful testimony! When we're overflowing with God's praises, there's no room for selfishness or pride. Offering praises to God can turn a difficult journey into one that's beautiful. Furthermore, God's praises are contagious to those who know Him. With a godly focus, humble spirit, and willingness to express our worship of Him, we can set off a chain reaction that brings others into a spirit of worship as Moses did.

If you were tasked with leading through the wilderness a large nation of God's chosen people comprised of hundreds of thousands of individuals who were rebellious and complainers, what would you ask of God? Superpowers? Influence? Here is what Moses requests: "Show me your way, that I may know you, that I may continue to find favor in your sight" (Exodus 33:13). He then begs to see God's glory (33:18). Moses realizes that in knowing God's character and experiencing His glory, he'll be able to live victoriously in the mission God has for him.

When we focus on learning God's desires through His character, and when we worship His glory, we walk in step with His Spirit and live victorious Christian lives, having everything necessary to accomplish His plan for our lives.

In the next chapter of Exodus, the Lord answers the request of Moses by passing before him and proclaims His name and attributes—excellent prompts for worship. Moses had asked to see God's glory, and God reveals this to him along with His name and attributes. God's glory, name, and attributes are all inextricably linked to each other.

Here is God's self-proclamation to Moses:

The LORD, the LORD, the compassionate and gracious God, slow to anger, and abounding in loyal love and faithfulness, keeping loyal love for thousands, forgiving iniquity and transgression and sin. But he by no means leaves the guilty unpunished, responding to the transgression of fathers by dealing with children and children's children, to the third and fourth generation. (Exodus 34:6-7)

What's the only response to experiencing God's glory? Moses "makes haste" to bow down to the ground and worship (34:8). Oh, that we would intensely desire to know God's ways and see His glory above all else. That's the issue. We don't need louder music, flashier lights, four-part harmonies, or better worship leaders. The longing pursuit of God's glory is enough.

In Deuteronomy 32 we read words Moses spoke near the time of his death. They're structured as a song of teaching, as Moses passes along a lifetime's worth of intimate knowledge of God. Of course, he doesn't merely say, "Don't hit rocks when you should speak to them; it doesn't end well." Rather, the song is full of worship and adoration of God. He instructs his spiritual progeny through worship and through elucidating God's character and dealings with mankind. Some of his last recorded words are worship.

Since we were created for worship, there's no greater joy than to fulfill our design well by living a life overflowing with God's praise. The highest honor we can achieve in this life is praise from the Lord for our life of worship to Him. Moses received this commendation. He's mentioned throughout Scripture for the various aspects of his worship life. His legacy recorded in the Bible was only partially the physical act of leading the children of Israel out of bondage. It was also knowing God face to face (Exodus 33:11; Numbers 12:7-8; Deuteronomy 34:10), bowing to God in humble service (Revelation 15:3; Hebrews 3:5; Joshua 1:1-2), and his enduring worship (Revelation 15).

The legacy of this worshipful song in Deuteronomy 32 is one that lasts into the end times. Not bad for a man who insisted so vehemently that he was slow of tongue and couldn't speak well. The worship that emerges from knowing God intimately and bowing our life to Him overrides the lack of skill with our tongues. Imagine what it would be like to hear your worship of God sung to Him at the end of all things by throngs of victorious Christians commissioned by God Himself to sing His praises? This is exactly the image we get in Revelation 15 as those who are victorious over the beast are given harps by God, and they sing "the song of Moses the servant of God and the song of the Lamb":

> *Great and astounding* are your deeds, Lord God, the All-Powerful! Just and true are your ways, King over the nations! Who will not fear you, O Lord, and glorify your name, because you alone are holy? All nations will come and worship before you for your righteous acts have been revealed. (Revelation 15:3-4)

Selah

And in the midst of the lampstands was one like a son of man. He was dressed in a robe extending down to his feet and he wore a wide golden belt around his chest. His head and hair were as white as wool, even as white as snow, and his eyes were like a fiery flame. His feet were like polished bronze refined in a furnace, and his voice was like the roar of many waters. He held seven stars in his right hand, and a sharp double-edged sword extended out of his mouth. His face shone like the sun shining at full strength. When I saw him I fell down at his feet as though I were dead, but he placed his right hand on me and said: "Do not be afraid! I am the first and the last, and the one who lives! I was dead, but look, now I am alive—forever and ever—and I hold the keys of death and of Hades!" (Revelation 1:13-18)

The LORD deserves praise, for he has heard my plea for mercy! The LORD strengthens and protects me; I trust in him with all my heart. I am rescued and my heart is full of joy; I will sing to him in gratitude. (Psalm 28:6-7)

David

When we think about David, we might recall individual events or specific passages of Scripture—such as 1 Samuel 13:14, where we read that David was a man after God's own heart (a description reiterated in Acts 13:22). We may think of David's fight with Goliath or of his sin with Bathsheba. Or we remember reading (in 1 Samuel 24) about David's temptation to destroy Saul, his victory over that temptation, his sensitive conscience, and his interest in God's cosmic plan rather than his own well-being.

All these stories tell us great things about David. In every pulpit and household in Christianity, David is recognized as a spiritual hero, and his great deeds are hailed. However, spiritual greatness comes not from deed or event but from the depth of communion of God's heart with our own. David was a man after God's own heart not because he defeated Goliath, or even because he had the courage to fight Goliath. It was because David's heart burned with a passion for God's glory to be made evident on earth. This was the same glory that Goliath was denigrating.

When we feel that our faith is under assault or that God's glory is being minimized, we sometimes respond inappropriately because we take the attack as being against us. We may sense that our views are becoming a minority, and we panic. Of course, this can lead people to do all sorts of irrational things, such as raging in arguments on social media or viewing the other side as the enemy rather than the lost whom God loves.

If you want God's glory to be exalted in all the earth, then build a lifestyle of overflowing worship. This was David's outlet of passion for God's glory.

When Goliath mocked God, the rage it prompted in David was not a sinking feeling that his theological views were in the minority. In fact, David's passion for God's glory caused him to be in the minority even among believers. His rage and passion did not cause him to merely sit back and fret or to rant to his fellow Israelites. His passion drove David to do great things. It blinded him to supposedly insurmountable odds because he knew God's power and God's zeal for His own glory.

David's passion for God's glory also drove him to write the most beautiful worship passages in Scripture. We see this passion clearly when we more closely examine what's written *by* him rather than what's written about him. Similarly, in examining our own spiritual lives, we're wise to assess not the things we've done for the Lord, or what others say about our spiritual maturity, but rather what our own hearts say of the Lord and His highness.

The Psalms are thick with worship. David (and others) wrote song after song elucidating and praising God's character and actions so that those of us who often struggle to croak out a short list of God's attributes in praise have an endless wealth of worship material.

Of course, David didn't confine his worship to pen and parchment. David twice danced and worshiped exuberantly before the ark of the covenant as it was transported, drawing scorn from his wife for his outward display of devotion (2 Samuel 6). David sat before the Lord and worshiped Him after God made His covenant with him (2 Samuel 7). He worshiped God after He delivered him (2 Samuel 22). He organized worshipers and led a worship service for the ceremony when the ark was back in the temple (1 Chronicles 16). He appointed and organized four thousand Levites for the sole purpose of praising God with their musical instruments and speaking praises from the Lord (1 Chronicles 23; 25). David praised the Lord in front of the entire congregation after a willing and generous offering was taken for building the temple (1 Chronicles 29).

David's worshipful response to God in 1 Chronicles 29 bears many lessons for us. Early in this chapter, the entire congregation is led into financial giving and worship by David's own sacrificial giving and humble worship. He isn't focused here on being a worship leader, but rather a leading worshiper.

In the church today, the moment we make "leader" the focus instead of "worshiper," we lose our intention. This is not to say that being a leader is a bad thing. A pastor must be a leader, focused both on God and on meeting the congregation's needs and helping them grow. However, a "worship leader" must be focused first and foremost on worshiping our magnificent God. No amount of poking and prodding, lights and smoke, layers of guitars, and repetitions of choruses will prompt a person or congregation to truly worship. Yes, these things may prompt a response from the congregation, but it will likely be an emotional one rather than a spiritual one.

The role of leading worshiper is an important one, because congregational preparation can truly help people come into a spirit of worship. When the congregation hears of God's glory from the Word, or hears truly worshipful text written and vocalized by someone awed by God's glory, it will do more to lead a group into worship than breathy singing or passionate instrumental accompaniment ever will.

This application comes in the form of congregational worship because that's the context with David, and also because it's easy for us to identify with and to visualize. But the application can also be for leading family worship or conversational worship. We'll fail in the leading part if we aren't focused on our own worshiping part. We can't expect to impress God's greatness on others if we don't bow before it ourselves.

David was gripped by God's glory in 1 Chronicles 29. The chapter starts with his recognition that building the temple is a great task, a task ultimately not for man but for the Lord God (29:1). The project was to be spectacular—not because everyone wanted it to look nice or to reflect well on themselves, but because they served a God magnificent beyond description. David supplies a sacrificial gift out of his own wealth beyond that which he has already inspired the people to give. It wasn't enough that he encourage others to give— he wanted to give of his own resources to worship the Lord. In response to his worshipful giving, a magnificent freewill offering ensued among the people. Then he praises the Lord.

In David's shoes, I might have been tempted to pat myself on the back and congratulate myself for leading the congregation in this service. More piously, David could have praised the congregation for their dedication to the Lord, making them feel entitled to God's favor. Don't we do that as well? We serve the Lord genuinely (or sometimes not), and then expect His favor. This expectation is clearly evidenced by our dismay when life becomes overwhelming to us, and we ask God, "Why, Lord? I've been serving You!"

David's response is different:

> *O LORD God of our father Israel, you deserve praise forevermore! O LORD, you are great, mighty, majestic, magnificent, glorious, and sovereign over all the sky and earth! You have dominion and exalt yourself as the ruler of all. You are the source of wealth and honor; you rule over all. You possess strength and might to magnify and give strength to all. Now, our God, we give thanks to you and praise your majestic name!*
>
> *But who am I and who are my people, that we should be in a position to contribute this much? Indeed, everything comes from you, and we have simply given back to you what is yours. For we are resident foreigners and nomads in your presence, like all our ancestors; our days are like a shadow on the earth, without security. O LORD our God, all this wealth, which we have collected to build a temple for you to honor your holy name, comes from you; it all belongs to you.* (1 Chronicles 29:10-16).

David really understood a principle that Jesus would later teach:

> *Would any one of you say to your slave who comes in from the field after plowing or shepherding sheep, "Come at once and sit down for a meal"? Won't the master instead say to him, "Get my dinner ready, and make yourself ready to serve me while I eat and drink. Then you may eat and*

drink"? He won't thank the slave because he did what he was told, will he? So you too, when you have done everything you were commanded to do, should say, "We are slaves undeserving of special praise; we have only done what was our duty." (Luke 17:7-10)

We don't deserve praise for piety in our giving and worship. Every word of true worship is only a return of God's gift to us in revealing His glory to us, just as David observes that everything comes from God and belongs to Him. That we should be so fortunate to be given the revelation of God's character and allowed to return worship to Him is beyond comprehension.

As David realizes these truths and prays them before the congregation in humble worship, the people are incited to worship. It's not, "Oh yeah, praise the Lord and pass the biscuits," but rather praising the Lord while bowing down and stretching out flat on the ground before Him (1 Chronicles 29:20).

One might suppose that worship came easily for him because his life was blessed immensely by the Lord. But remember all the reality of David's life. It wasn't long after he was anointed as king by Samuel, and after he'd killed Goliath and become vastly popular in Israel, that David was a man on the run. He had spears thrown at him multiple times; he was betrayed, lied to, and surrounded in the wilderness by enemies. He fled from cave to cave in the wilderness. He begged for food from the priest and feigned insanity before a foreign king. He lived in exile among Israel's mortal enemies, the Philistines. David was constantly running for his life. He easily could have focused on the trials—on the wind and the waves—rather than on God.

Many of his psalms were written during this time. Yes, there's hardship and questioning in these songs, but also joyful praise and acknowledgment of the Lord's character.

With the many psalms David wrote and all his exuberant worship of the Lord recorded throughout Scripture, we can easily see David's passion for God's glory. Even the passing of his scepter to Solomon was done with praise to God and without self-exaltation for his successful political career. Some of his last public words are these: "The LORD God of Israel is worthy of praise because today he has placed a successor on my throne and allowed me to see it" (1 Kings 1:48).

What a blessing it would be to have our last words on this earth be the worship of our God before we're ushered into His presence! David's life shows us what it's like to be someone after God's own heart—to worship Him in life, in battle, in hardship, in victory, in defeat, and at all other times.

Hannah

How often have you told the Lord, "If you'll only do what I ask you this once, then I'll (fill in the blank)"? Hannah tells that to the Lord in 1 Samuel 1. She vows that if God gives her a son, she'll dedicate him to the Lord for service in the temple for the entirety of his life. God grants Hannah's request, and she's faithful to fulfill her vow.

One might expect Hannah's song of worship to come at the time of Samuel's birth. Interestingly, it comes instead as she's giving the boy Samuel to the Lord and leaving him in the care of Eli, never to come under her care again. Although her song (recorded in 1 Samuel 2) is filled with worship and joy, I suspect that Hannah is inwardly struggling at the end of chapter 1. She has waited for this son her whole life. Her rival, Peninnah, has been harassing her and rejoicing over Hannah's misfortune. Hannah has suffered scorn from those close to her. Now she has a son who she's about to leave with Eli, functionally returning to her childless state. Her maternal instinct is likely pressing her as well. Yet, she worships.

The last time my older brother and I ever wrestled together ended with me pushing him through the wall. Not our greatest moment. To make matters worse, my parents were sitting right in front of us watching. They calmly informed us that we would be paying for the repair, but when the repairmen heard the story, they just laughed and charged us for materials only. Like that wall, we all have cracks and holes in our lives. Some of them develop slowly over time, some happen quickly, and some are a result of someone else putting their rear end through our emotional or spiritual wall.

We're told to give thanks "in everything" (1 Thessalonians 5:18); our worship is not to happen only when our circumstances seem to be going well. So how do we worship when we're full of cracks and holes?

Hannah shows us how in 1 Samuel 2. She's more focused on her Savior than on her current struggle. She doesn't plead with God to allow her to go back on her promise. Rather, she recounts her theology and details how the Lord acts according to His attributes:

> **My heart** has rejoiced in the LORD… Indeed I rejoice in your deliverance. No one is holy like the LORD! There is no one other than you! There is no rock like our God! (2:1-2)

She worships His sovereignty in all situations:

> **The LORD** both kills and gives life; he brings down to the grave and raises up.
>
> The LORD impoverishes and makes wealthy; he humbles and he exalts. He lifts the weak from the dust; he raises the poor from the ash heap to seat them with princes and to bestow on them an honored position.
>
> The foundations of the earth belong to the LORD, and he has placed the world on them. (2:6-8)

She finishes with prophecy concerning the Messiah (the first time this term is used in the Bible), showing her confidence that her Lord holds the future:

He will strengthen his king and exalt the power of his anointed one. (2:10)

So this is how we worship in all situations—by rejoicing in the Lord, knowing His attributes, and remembering His promises. Hannah worshiped despite the big hole in her life. Rather than becoming bitter, she plugged and reinforced the wall with God's attributes and promises, and painted it over with the beautiful vibrancy of worship.

Selah

"To whom can you compare me? Whom do I resemble?" says the Holy One.

Look up at the sky! Who created all these heavenly lights?

He is the one who leads out their ranks; he calls them all by name. Because of his absolute power and awesome strength, not one of them is missing.

Why do you say, Jacob, Why do you say, Israel, "The LORD is not aware of what is happening to me, My God is not concerned with my vindication"?
(Isaiah 40:25-27)

I give them eternal life, and they will never perish; no one will snatch them from my hand. My Father, who has given them to me, is greater than all, and no one can snatch them from my Father's hand. The Father and I are one. (John 10:28-30)

Mary

If you struggle in your worship life, try memorizing the words of worship spoken by others. The Bible is full of passages of beautiful worship, and they're recorded there to aid our worship.

Along with our joining voices in corporate worship, one of the main functions of Sunday morning worship is to have a ready supply of worship material for our private worship lives. For our personal growth, memorizing and repeating the passage of Hannah's prayer from 1 Samuel 2 would likely benefit us more than repeating phrases from a modern chorus on autopilot. Mary did that—and so much more. She used not only Hannah's prayer, but also several passages from the Psalms. She knew the Scriptures well—she was a student of the Word in both head and heart. Mary knew what true worship was, and she knew plenty of it. She made this legacy of worship her own, and she used all of what she knew from the Word to form her own beautiful prayer of praise to the Lord.

In Luke 1, we find the account of the angel's announcement to Mary that she would give birth to the Messiah. Her response to the angel points to Mary's preeminent spiritual qualities—submission and faith. She said, "Yes, I am a servant of the Lord; let this happen to me according to your word" (1:38).

After this, Mary went to visit her cousin Elizabeth. Upon hearing Elizabeth's blessing upon Mary and her child, Mary burst forth in worship:

> *My soul exalts the Lord, and my spirit has begun to rejoice in God my Savior, because he has looked upon the humble state of his servant.*
>
> *For from now on all generations will call me blessed, because he who is mighty has done great things for me, and holy is his name; from generation to generation he is merciful to those who fear him.*

He has demonstrated power with his arm; he has scattered those whose pride wells up from the sheer arrogance of their hearts.

He has brought down the mighty from their thrones, and has lifted up those of lowly position; he has filled the hungry with good things, and has sent the rich away empty.

He has helped his servant Israel, remembering his mercy, as he promised to our ancestors, to Abraham and to his descendants forever. (1:46-55)

Note the similarities between Hannah's and Mary's prayers. Both rejoice in the Lord. They both worship His holiness, sovereignty, justice, mercy, provision, and attention to the lowly. Hannah references the Messiah, and Mary references her Savior. What's most important, however, is that from the beginning of their prayers we see both women worshiping from their hearts. Hannah isn't focusing on her impending loneliness, nor Mary on her potential social ostracization. Neither are they merely expressing gratitude for the blessing of a child. Their hearts recognize the goodness and splendor of their King, and they don't hold back their expressions.

Mary's beautiful heart was full of worship, and she'd hidden passages of worship from the Word in her heart. There's no indication that she sat down and penned this prayer of praise. She was familiar enough using the Scriptures in prayer that she could speak them to others as the Spirit led her to.

When we offer worship, we must get over ourselves and what we sound like. If we stutter, or we're not creative, we should learn passages of worship from Scripture. Like the song of Moses—which has been immortalized in Scripture and will be used in the end times—Mary's "Magnificat" has been immortalized through the millennia as a clear window to the worshipful soul of the mother of Christ. As we often see in Scripture, the worship we offer has lasting value.

Study Questions

1. Have you ever found yourself worshiping a godly teacher or musician? Can you think of a time in life when you allowed others to do your seeking of God for you?

2. How can you tell stories of God's work in your life, as Moses did—stories that cause others around you to worship Him?

3. Are you passionate about God's glory? If so, what are some constructive outlets for that passion, besides worship?

Chapter 10
Worship and the Fear of the Lord

Fear is reverence, fear is awe, fear is terror—the debate continues as to which of these the fear of the Lord actually is. But the fear of the Lord is all three of them—awe, reverence, and terror—as we see when we interpret the Scriptures accurately and as a whole.

We know of course that anyone who has placed faith in Christ for the forgiveness of sins is spared from the wrath of God. Why then should that person have a fear of God that is in part terror? Scripture makes it clear that there's an element of terror in the fear of God, even for His children whom He dearly loves. Should we walk away from Him in sin, His chastisement of us may be severe and dreadful, sometimes leading to death.

Also, consider Hebrews 10, which speaks of those who "deliberately keep on sinning after receiving the knowledge of truth" (10:26) and compares such a person with "someone who rejected the law of Moses" (10:28):

> *How much greater punishment do you think that person deserves who has contempt for the Son of God, and profanes the blood of the covenant that made him holy, and insults the Spirit of grace? For we know the one who said, "Vengeance is mine, I will repay," and again, "The Lord will judge his people." It is a terrifying thing to fall into the hands of the living God. (10:29-31)*

Although God's children—saved by His grace, sanctified by Christ's blood, and sealed by the Holy Spirit—need not fear the fires of hell, we still would be wise to stand in reverence, awe, and terror of Him. The Greek word used most commonly in the New Testament for fear has *phobos* as the root. This is the same root from which we get our English word phobia, which commonly implies terror or dread. In the Bible, *phobos* is used for the terror that seized the disciples when they saw Jesus and thought He was a ghost (Matthew 14:26), for the reverence with which we're to share the defense of our faith (1 Peter 3:15), and for the awe that came over the early church as the Spirit of God worked wonders among them (Acts 2:43).

The fear of God has many aspects and facets. Logically, since God's character is complex, our interaction with His character must also be complex and sometimes not easily understood. How do we fear Him who calls us by name and loves us intimately? How can we call the King of the universe "Daddy"? Why do we fear Him if there's now no condemnation to those who are in Christ?

Like many theological questions for which an answer must be attempted but cannot be fully discovered, these questions should be welcomed rather than shunned. They help build up our knowledge of God. Through meditating on Scripture and worshiping God for His revealed nature, we understand more facets of His character. Our knowledge of Him becomes more thorough and unified rather than fragmented.

So much of the Bible is devoted to the fear of God that we need only study the Scriptures to see the many facets of fearing God, rather than trying to fit a definition into a single sentence. Perhaps it's more important to understand what the fear of God does than attempting to pin down a single definition.

What the Fear of God Does

The fear of God grips us. It seizes us. It commands our attention and intensifies our walk with Him. Without fear of God, we see His glorious attributes only in vague, faded colors. With fear, we see them in intense, electric colors.

With God's fear, we cannot be complacent. Before salvation, the fear of the Lord was the impetus to cry out for Him to save us from our sins. Now the fear of the Lord is the impetus to obey Him and worship Him. Without this driving force, our spiritual lives will be bleak and half-hearted. Church will be a social meet. Our time in the Word will be academic. Our prayer times will feel like we're talking only to ourselves. Our conduct will be similar to that of the moralist standing beside us.

Likewise, the fear of the Lord is a crucial presence for true worship. Worship without fear leads to what's warned about throughout Scripture—lip service without a lifestyle of obedience and devotion. It's something that God decries:

> *These people say they are loyal to me; they say wonderful things about me, but they are not really loyal to me. Their worship consists of nothing but man-made ritual.* (Isaiah 29:13)

It's no coincidence that the fear of God is paired with worship and praise in many Scripture verses. Fear of God without worship that's based in Spirit and in truth is pagan spiritualism. Worship without fear is a checked box. A six-week goal that goes two weeks. A kick. Dangerously casual.

Several years ago, I had the pleasure of befriending an esteemed and godly pastor who really knew the heart of God. He was always patient and welcoming, eager to talk and discuss things of God with younger generations, who mostly viewed him as an older and respected friend. In his congregation, there was a young man who was zealous about many things of God, often to the point of argument without wisdom or reverence. Because of the pastor's graciousness and warmth, this young man would engage him in debate with the same level of respect (which was sometimes disrespect) that he might have for a peer. Those standing nearby cringed at the relative impertinence of this young man in contrast to the gracious replies of the wise older pastor. It was a classic example of familiarity without respect.

We do the same in our relationship with God. We sometimes approach Him with over-familiarity because He graciously invites us to come boldly into His very throne room. Of course He loves us as children and delights in our relationship with Him. But that's only because He allows us to be His children by His grace that demanded His own Son to be crushed. If we say God is our friend, it's only because He allows His infinite riches to be lavished on us, and not because we belong to some club that gives us VIP access.

Familiarity with God can become blasphemous if not felt in the setting of fear. Because of this, some facet of fear must be present at all times when we approach the Lord, even when we approach Him as a crying child approaches his father to climb on his lap and be comforted. The psalmist asks, "If You, LORD, should mark iniquities, O Lord, who could stand? But there is forgiveness with You, that You may be feared" (Psalm 130:3-4 NASB). Even the Lord's forgiveness of us should cause us to fear Him with reverence. We don't deserve His forgiveness, nor do we understand the horror of our sins and extent of His forgiveness. But experiencing His forgiveness should drive us to fear Him and worship Him as much when we confess our sins today as it did when we first confessed our sin and need for a Savior at the time of salvation. As Charles Spurgeon wrote,

> Wonder at God's merciful love is a very practical emotion. Holy wonder will lead you to grateful worship and heartfelt thanksgiving. It will cause within you godly watchfulness; you will be afraid to sin against such a love as this.

While few if any of us have directly experienced God's splendor of holiness in the way Isaiah did, all of us who are believers have experienced His forgiveness. So let's never excuse ourselves from knowing His fear because we haven't experienced Him.

Those words in Psalm 130:3-4 also help us understand a vital principle in our study and worship of God—that each of God's attributes must be viewed in light of His other attributes. When pondering the forgiveness and mercy shown by human beings, there isn't much to be feared. In fact, human mercy and forgiveness may sometimes even be seen negatively as weakness or pandering. Contrast that with what David Guzik writes about God's mercy in his commentary on Romans 2:

The riches of God's mercy may be measured by four considerations:

His greatness—to wrong a great man is a great wrong, and God is greatest of all—yet He shows mercy.

His omniscience—if someone knew *all* our sin, would they show mercy? Yet God shows mercy.

His power—sometimes wrongs are not settled because they are out of our power, yet God is able to settle every wrong against Him—yet He's rich in mercy.

The object of His mercy: mere man—would we show mercy to an ant? Yet God is rich in mercy.

When we consider God's mercy in light of His greatness, omniscience, and power, and in light of our own lowliness, His mercy is truly something to be feared. Similarly, His love (an attribute that in human terms does not provoke fear), when considered in light of His holiness, justice, and righteousness, is something we cannot begin to fathom, though our eternity depends on it.

The fear of God not only grips us, but should also push us toward Him through worship and obedience. Imagine a large magnet that exerts a powerful field. We, as small magnets, will either be pushed away from this powerful magnet or drawn toward it. In this analogy, God is the magnet, and His fear is the magnetic force. If our walk with the Lord is characterized by obedience and worship, His fear will draw us to Himself. If we're inwardly rotting because of sin, our fear of God will push us away from Him.

This can be seen in the Scriptures in the first mention of fear—when Adam, after he sinned, first responds to God: "I heard you moving about in the orchard, and I was afraid because I was naked, so I hid." (Genesis 3:10). Adam's sin caused him to become afraid and to hide from God. He was fearful because his sinful soul was naked before a holy and righteous God, even as the shame of his physical nakedness was realized. When he could no longer run away from God, he tried to redirect God's attention toward Eve's actions in an attempt to quell his own fear.

Jonah knew the fear of the Lord. We see this throughout his story. First, he declares that he's a Hebrew and that he worships the Lord, the God of heaven who made the sea and land (Jonah 1:9).

Second, his prayer from the belly of the great fish is beautifully worshipful. In it, Jonah reverently praises God for His willingness to answer and His omnipresence (2:1), His sovereignty and omnipotence (2:2), His salvation (2:6,9), and His mercy (2:8). Things were looking pretty bleak for Jonah, being in the digestive chamber of a large fish many feet below the surface of the sea. But he promises God that he'll offer sacrifices to Him with a public declaration of praise—not on the condition that God delivers him, but in confident knowledge of God's power and plan. Jonah obviously fears God more than he fears the belly of the fish. This is how the fear of God and worship should interrelate: knowledge of God causing the fear of God, leading to the worship of God.

Third, after Jonah witnesses the repentance of the people of Nineveh, he prays this:

Oh, Lord, this is just what I thought would happen when I was in my own country. This is what I tried to prevent by attempting to escape to Tarshish! —because I knew that you are gracious and compassionate, slow to anger and abounding in mercy, and one who relents concerning threatened judgment. (4:2)

Remember Psalm 130:4: "There is forgiveness with you, that you may be feared." Jonah felt the force of God's graciousness, compassion, and mercy to such a degree that he ran away from God. He feared God's graciousness toward his enemies to the extent that it caused Jonah to run away—not from Nineveh, but from the Lord (1:3,10). Because of the sinful bitterness in his heart toward his enemies, his fear of the Lord drove him *away* from God in both the beginning and ending of the book, while in the middle, the fear of the Lord drove him *toward* God through worship and obedience.

The wonderful thing about the fear of God is that not only does it turn us toward God, but God turns Himself toward those who fear Him. This is different from a human king craving power for his own ego. Human fear places a divide between the one feared and the one fearing. The greater that divide, the more perceived power the ruler has, with less chance of rebellion or treason. A magistrate who desires the fear of the masses is unlikely to reach out in love and desire to those masses, since it could lessen the divide.

In the 1959 movie *Ben-Hur*, the young and ambitious Messala finds himself tasked with ruling the unrestful Roman territory of Judea. Eager to establish himself, he condemns his childhood friend Judah Ben-Hur for a crime that Messala knows Ben-Hur did not commit. "By making this example of you," he says, "I discourage treason. By condemning without hesitation an old friend, I shall be feared." We're not so different from that, even today in our culture of faux peace. We fear not being feared. We do whatever's necessary to have respect and not be mocked. We insulate ourselves with friends who tell us what we want to hear. We tend to give the gospel only to those nice people who "would make good Christians," and pass over those we deem unlikely to trust Christ. If there's any question of whether we'll be feared or respected, we tend to run away or threaten to increase that fear or respect.

God is so different. In how we relate to Him, there's a constant threat that we'll replace fear with familiarity and respect with presumption. Yet He never threatens us or runs from us. To the contrary, He turns toward those who fear Him and worship Him, as the prophet Malachi points out:

> *Then those who feared the LORD spoke to one another, and the LORD gave attention and heard it, and a book of remembrance was written before Him for those who fear the LORD and who esteem His name. "They will be Mine," says the LORD of hosts, "on the day that I prepare My own possession, and I will spare them as a man spares his own son who serves him."* (Malachi 3:16-17 NASB)

And note these words from David:

> *Who is the man who fears the LORD? He will instruct him in the way he should choose. His soul will abide in prosperity, And his descendants will inherit the land. The secret of the LORD is for those who fear Him, And He will make them know His covenant.* (Psalm 25:12-14 NASB)

What is it that the Lord confides to us? Knowledge of His glory. Wisdom regarding His workings. Understanding of His attributes. Acknowledging the Holy One is understanding (Proverbs 9:10). It's a beautiful cycle: We drink in the Scriptures, meditating on God's Word as it creates our awe and fear of Him; we worship Him in holy reverence; then He reveals still more of Himself to us through His Word.

It may seem counterintuitive that the fear of God brings us closer to Him, and Him to us. But when you experience this cycle, it's more wonderful than strange.

In what direction is the fear of the Lord turning you? Are you hearing the voice of the Lord in His Word, then falling to your knees in adoration? Does this compel you to share your faith with others so that they may experience the goodness of God and be spared from His wrath? Or does it rather cause you to run away from God by insulating yourself with comfort and protection, so that you fail to hear God's call to missions? Does it cause you to contrive complex social and theological arguments that allow you to ignore God's command for you to help the poor?

God wants your respect and awe. He wants you to know Him so well that you're terrified of His greatness. He wants to turn toward you in relationship as you fear Him, whispering wisdom into your ear and transforming you into His likeness.

Selah

Sing to the LORD, you faithful followers of his; give thanks to his holy name.

For his anger lasts only a brief moment, and his good favor restores one's life.

One may experience sorrow during the night, but joy arrives in the morning…you turned my lament into dancing; you removed my sackcloth and covered me with joy. (Psalm 30:4-5,11)

This is what the LORD, your protector, says, the one who formed you in the womb: "I am the LORD, who made everything, who alone stretched out the sky, who fashioned the earth all by myself, who frustrates the omens of the empty talkers and humiliates the

omen readers, who overturns the counsel of the wise
men and makes their advice seem foolish.
(Isaiah 44:24-25)

Driven to the Ground

When the fear of the Lord grips us, it drives us not only toward
Him but also to the ground. If it's awe, we're driven to the ground in
adulation. If it's terror, we woefully fall to the ground in submission,
giving thanks that we don't experience His wrath. If it's reverence,
we bow before Him in humility and worship. This is where the fear
of the Lord and worship intersect.

Remember *proskyneo*? Kissing the ground. As believers, fear and
worship work together to place us in our proper orientation (on the
ground at God's footstool), doing what we were created to do in
singing God's praises.

Worship and fear also intersect at the foot of the cross. There, we
see the Creator of the universe, all of God's divine power wrapped
in human form, displayed to us by a sinless life, power over nature,
and the very voice of God. He was willingly stripped of His heavenly
glory and came to earth humbly, compelled by love to redeem His
own creation. He taught us from the infinite stores of heavenly
wisdom. Though a King, He served. He poured out love when
scorned. He blessed though cursed. With all the power to utterly
destroy mankind for self-preservation, instead He allowed the weak
to take His life. God's greatest gift to mankind was rejected. He
endured the bitterness of becoming sin and taking the fury of God's
wrath so that we can justly be forgiven.

He washed and cleansed us, not leaving us in our former sin. He
calls us His brothers. He sent us the Comforter, the Holy Spirit to seal
us and guide us through life. He's preparing mansions for us in
heaven with an unimaginable inheritance. He'll battle Satan and
ultimately defeat him for all time, along with vanquishing sin and
death permanently. This eternal timeline is represented in a single

snapshot at the foot of the cross. How can we not fear Him and worship Him?

At the end of this side of eternity, before time itself is wiped out, we see eternity heralded in, as God carries out the final restoration of creation to His originally intended purpose. And we see *phobos* and *proskyneo* used together:

> *Then I saw* another angel flying directly overhead, and he had an eternal gospel to proclaim to those who live on the earth—to every nation, tribe, language, and people. He declared in a loud voice: "Fear God and give him glory, because the hour of his judgment has arrived, and worship the one who made heaven and earth, the sea and the springs of water!" (Revelation 14:6-7)

> *Who* will not fear you, O Lord, and glorify your name, because you alone are holy? All nations will come and worship before you for your righteous acts have been revealed. (Revelation 15:4)

But even before creation is restored, we're commanded while still on this earth, "You who fear the Lord, praise him!" (Psalm 22:23). The fear of the Lord is inextricably linked to true worship.

This mixture of fear and worship seems counterintuitive in today's culture of on-demand worship songs—songs that sometimes carelessly promote self-fixation or an anthropocentric view of God. We need to recalibrate. Coming into His presence needs to be more about His fear and worship than merely jamming out to good tunes that give an artificial feeling of closeness to God.

What are the words we're singing to Him? Many "songs of worship" contain words and ideas that glorify self above God, or that don't line up with the teachings of Scripture. There's no catchy tune or single line of a song that can justify careless worship that causes us to focus on ourselves, or that goes against Scripture.

We're told, "Serve the LORD with fear and rejoice with trembling" (Psalm 2:11 KJV). We must evaluate ourselves. Do we fear the Lord? How can we tell?

The thing we fear in life becomes the thing to which we sacrifice our time, energy, resources, and words—and this is worship. It can be God, or it can be anything in the world that isn't God. We may fear missing out by living beneath a certain lifestyle, so we buy toys and expensive health products, while missionaries must come home because of financial shortages.

Conversely, if I fear God and understand that He wants me to love my wife in a way that represents well Christ's relationship with the church, I'll devote my energy to finding ways to show my love for her as Christ shows His love for the church. There are an infinite number of ways this plays out—both healthy ways of fearing God and worshiping Him, and also unhealthy ways of fearing anything else and worshiping it.

So how do we fear the Lord? Like pinning down a succinct definition of the fear of the Lord, it's difficult to nail down a step-by-step process for adequately fearing the Lord. A strong start can be found by considering this verse: "Praise the LORD! How blessed is the man who fears the LORD, who greatly delights in His commandments" (Psalm 112:1 NASB). The Hebrew style of poetry frequently uses pairs of lines with parallel meaning, so in this verse we see that fearing the Lord is essentially equated with delighting in His commandments. What then is delighting in His commandments? It's opening God's Word joyfully and expectantly. It's bowing to His kingdom before we bow to our online presence. It's being so glad to observe what He tells us that we forget the time. It's taking His Word with us throughout the day.

When we delight in His commandments, we find that His ways are perfect. His attributes become more clear to us as we carefully obey Him. We see His love for us when we refuse the false promises of sin in order to find the abundant joy that holiness brings. God is no killjoy. His precious commandments are not grievous but rather life-giving. In His love, He provides us with commandments that keep us from the rot of sin and bring us vibrant life.

We see His justice when we don't render evil for evil. In refraining, we free ourselves from bitterness, and we see God's recompense to those who have wronged us as they deal with consequences of their sin. We see His mercy in the same situation as He heals our wounds.

We see His faithfulness to draw near to us when we delight to draw near to Him.

As we see His attributes in motion on a day-to-day basis as we delight in His Word, we learn that His ways are infinitely superior to our own. We learn that we cannot reason our way through life, and that complete and utter submission to Him is our only true and right path.

Wisdom can be defined as seeing the world through the lens of Scripture. From this, Proverbs 2:1-7 makes sense. Paraphrased, it states that those who seek wisdom will begin to know the fear of the Lord, for the Lord gives wisdom to those who live righteously. The knowledge of God followed by the practice of God's laws leads to a deeper and more intricate knowledge of Him. This is where His fear is found. It isn't found singularly in a volume of theology. Nor is it found in the absent-minded mish-mush of moral living.

So we see clearly how the fear of the Lord is the beginning of wisdom. We delight in His commands and see His attributes as we live according to His ways. This allows us a much deeper view of the world around us as we seek to apply God's Word to every situation in our lives and to see His attributes in His workings.

Conversely, when we look to ourselves and human reasoning to get through life, we foolishly turn away from the fear of the Lord. This includes situational ethics, being too involved in the Lord's work to have intimacy with the Lord, allowing the world's influences (music, media, commentary) into our thinking, coming to Scripture with careless interpretations that are human-derived or emotion-driven, and many other ways.

> *Trust in the LORD with all your heart, and do not rely on your own understanding. Acknowledge him in all your ways, and he will make your paths straight. Do not be wise in your own estimation; fear the LORD and turn away from evil.* (Proverbs 3:5-7)

In this passage, the Hebrew parallels once again relate the commandment to not be wise in our own eyes with the commandment to fear the Lord. Whether intentionally or unintentionally, whether we're a survivalist or a comfort-lover, by plowing through life relying on our own resources we begin to ignore the fear of the Lord. One of the many dangers of this is that we become unable to hear His whispers, leaving Him no other choice but to communicate with us through His megaphone.

Imagine a powerful magistrate speaking to a mass of cheering people. He need only signal with his hand that he's about to speak, and the cheering crowd falls silent. We don't want to be that individual who doesn't recognize the gesture or respect the one making it. We don't want to be subjected to His megaphone. Though His megaphone is used in love for His children who don't fear Him, it's uncomfortable for us at best, and fatal at worst.

At the end of all things, every one of us will fear the Lord greatly, even if we don't right now. Those of us who are His redeemed will fear His great power, holiness, love, and mercy. Those who aren't redeemed will fear His power, holiness, wrath, and judgment.

> *So they will fear the name of the LORD from the west And His glory from the rising of the sun, For He will come like a rushing stream, Which the wind of the Lord drives.* (Isaiah 59:19 NASB)

Like a dazzling light which stuns eyes that are used to darkness, God's glory will be less distressing to us if we gaze on Him with fear and trembling through worship throughout this life.

The fear of the Lord can be found only at great cost: total surrender to His lordship. But as we journey through our walk of faith, worship, and obedience, we find that the cost is actually the reward. We were created to live in His fear. This is what He wants for us—that "He will be your sure foundation, providing a rich store of salvation, wisdom, and knowledge. The fear of the LORD will be your treasure" (Isaiah 33:6 NLT). We trade our shackles—the fear of man—for the comforting rod and staff that is the fear of God. The deeper we go in the fear of the Lord, the deeper and more vibrant our worship life will be.

Study Questions

1. What are characteristics of your life when you're fearing God? What is your life like when you're not fearing God?

2. How does the fear of the Lord help us turn away from human reasoning to submit to His Word?

3. Read Ecclesiastes 12:13. How does this compare to the following famous statement from the Westminster Shorter Catechism: "Man's chief end is to glorify God, and to enjoy him forever."

Chapter 11
Through the Lens of Charis

The eye is a remarkable bit of God's creation. Light is focused as it enters through the cornea, as peripheral rays are blocked by the iris. The light is focused again by the lens, then passes through a clear vitreous to form an image on the ninth of ten layers of the retina, where photoreceptors transmit that light via electrical signals to the brain. If our lens isn't working properly, what we see is in some way distorted or out of focus. If the light isn't focused well on the photoreceptors, but instead is focused in front of the retina, that's myopia (or nearsightedness). If the light is focused behind the retina, that's hyperopia (farsightedness). If the lens is cloudy, as in a cataract, the light is scattered, making colors look washed out and causing glare.

Interestingly, this system is so intricate and finely tuned that the lens must adjust even to focus different colors. Red, being a relatively long wavelength of visible light, doesn't change its angle when refracted as easily as blue does, and therefore needs more refracting power than blue. So it's possible to focus on green and have red out of focus, or focus on red and have blue look fuzzy.

The Greek word *charis* is the lens that helps us properly focus on God. There are two main branches of this word's meaning. The "incoming" usage of the word is translated "grace" in the New Testament (appearing as such about 130 times). This grace is the undeserved favor God bestows on us—both when we trust Him as our Savior and subsequently in our walk with Him.

The "outgoing" usage of *charis* is translated as "thanks" or "thanksgiving." It can be coupled with the Greek root *eu*, which implies the giving of thanks (from which we get "eucharist"). It's also found coupled with the word *homologeo*, which specifies an expression of thanks. When God's grace (*charis*) comes into focus for us at the time of salvation or in our walk with Him, we overflow with thanks (*charis*) back to Him.

When we see all the elements of our relationship with God through the focusing lens of His grace, which results in an outpouring of gratitude, we experience Him the way we're intended to. For example, God places us in the body of Christ with other believers. When we see and encounter those brothers and sisters in Christ through the focusing lens of grace with the response of thanksgiving, then true love and fellowship abide in the church.

There's a similar process producing worship in our lives. God shines His attributes inwardly upon us through revelation of His Word and creation. We focus our understanding of those attributes through grace and thanksgiving, and outward worship bursts forth. This is a colossal truth that will drastically change our relationship with God, as Paul indicates:

> *As God's grace* [charis] reaches more and more people, there will be great thanksgiving [*eucharistia*], and God will receive more and more glory. (2 Corinthians 4:15)

So here it is: *charis* in, *charis* out. The abundant grace of God shining into our lives, and the overflowing thanksgiving pouring out of us. And when thanksgiving overflows, the glory of God reflects from our lives and floods every dark corner around us. This is worship that's true and responsive.

Interestingly, the trigger for grace to reach more and more is found in Paul's prior words in verse 13: "We believe, therefore we speak." There's a potent administration of grace to believers through speaking about the Lord to each other. That's why Hebrews 10:25

tells us to not forsake the assembling of ourselves together, but to encourage one another. Christians aren't meant to live in a vacuum. We cannot be loners in the faith and be spiritually healthy.

Furthermore, we shouldn't routinely neglect encouraging other believers in the faith. How common it is for us to take for granted this opportunity to distribute God's grace to each other through worship and the Word, while we instead settle for small talk. Consider this instruction from Paul:

> *Let the word of Christ richly dwell within you, with all wisdom teaching and admonishing one another with psalms and hymns and spiritual songs, singing with thankfulness in your hearts to God.* (Colossians 3:16 NASB)

This is the body of Christ at its finest! The message of Christ dwells in us, continually making its abode there. We cannot have fellowship apart from Christ and His message. Through wisdom (we must worship in spirit *and* in truth), we encourage each other with psalms, hymns, and spiritual songs. The result? An outpouring of gratitude to God! This is another great example of "*charis* in" by Christ's message (the gospel of grace), and "*charis* out" with thanksgiving to God. This happens among the body of believers when the Word and worship are spoken to each other through the lens of *charis*.

When We Don't Use the Charis Lens

Here's an example given by Paul of the failure to use the *charis* lens:

> *For since the creation of the world his invisible attributes — his eternal power and divine nature — have been clearly seen, because they are understood through what has been made. So people are without excuse. For although they knew God,*

they did not glorify him as God or give him thanks but they became futile in their thoughts and their senseless hearts were darkened. (Romans 1:20-21)

The *charis* lens ceases to function when we don't *recognize* God's grace as it's revealed to us. God displays His attributes to all people through creation. The inward pathway is there, as God in His grace shows Himself to all mankind. But they fail to glorify God or give Him thanks. The outgoing pathway is missing.

This is of course the first step of the downward spiral detailed in the rest of Romans 1. When we fail to worship God and give Him thanks, we make ourselves vulnerable to pride and self-sufficiency, which are deadly. Just as when a severe cataract darkens the vision in our eyes because it has opacified our lens, so our spiritual hearts become darkened when the lens of *charis* ceases to function properly because we don't recognize God's grace.

The *charis* lens can also be hindered when we fail to *accept* God's grace. The Pharisees worshiped God, but their worship fell short. They didn't focus God's attributes through grace and thanksgiving, but rather changed God's attributes into a burden for others or a means for their own personal gain. When we receive God's truth and don't apply grace and thanksgiving to it, our spiritual eyesight is out of focus, or reveals only washed-out colors. We may be able to see His holiness clearly, but His love is out of focus for us, making us heartless and legalistic. Or His love for the poor and sick may be clear, while His reconciliatory desire for them may be out of focus for us when we assume that the gospel might offend them. Again, like a cataract in our physical eyes, the clarity of God's glory may appear washed out to us if grace and thanksgiving are stifled by our sin or dullness of spirit. When God is in focus, and His attributes dazzle us with their vibrancy, thanksgiving and worship will pour out.

Spiritual Barbecue Sauce

God's administering of His grace to us is not episodic but

continuous, as Charles Spurgeon eloquently describes:

> Every hour, yea, every moment has brought a favor upon its wings. Look downward and give thanks, for you are saved from hell; look on the right hand and give thanks, for you are enriched with gracious gifts; look on the left hand and give thanks, for you are shielded from deadly ills; look above you and give thanks, for heaven awaits you.

The inward flow of God's grace is constantly streaming to us. And when the lens of *charis* is functional, we're constantly receiving that grace, and our thanksgiving pours out constantly rather than episodically. This is the secret behind the command in 1 Thessalonians 5:18: "In everything give thanks. For this is God's will for you in Christ Jesus."

The secret to giving thanks continually is to use God's continuous grace to focus all circumstances in our lives. As we do that, worshipful thanksgiving will flow. So just as God's grace applies to us in all things in all circumstances, thanksgiving can be used in all things in all circumstances.

At our house, there are usually at least two different bottles of barbecue sauce in the refrigerator. Barbecue sauce makes almost everything taste better. You can pour the sauce on it, fry it in sauce, bake it in sauce, marinate it in sauce, or even just eat the sauce. Eggs, sandwiches, mac and cheese, tacos, vegetables, casseroles, pot roasts, hot dogs, hamburgers—you name it, and barbecue sauce makes it better! For some, it may be ketchup from which no food is safe. One of my favorite things about eating with my Mexican friends and family is the delicious salsa (a close second for me to barbecue sauce) that finds its way onto nearly everything as well. Regardless of where you're from, most regions have a sauce that makes everything better. Thanksgiving is that sauce for the Christian life.

Philippians 4:6-7 states that prayer and supplication are much better with a helping of thanksgiving. It's the antidote to worry, and it ushers in God's peace. Thanksgiving is a crucial ingredient in prayer and supplication, because without thanksgiving, prayer and supplication can be offered in an attitude of worry. Drowning our prayers and supplications in the thanksgiving sauce shows us that we're using the *charis* lens to focus God's attribute of benevolence toward us as our Provider.

Colossians 3:17 tells us, "Whatever you do, whether in word or deed, do it all in the name of the Lord Jesus, giving thanks to God the Father through him." All our daily activities and conversations should be marinated with thanksgiving. At work, even the scutwork assigned to you should be done with thanksgiving. The lunchtime conversations should be filled with thanksgiving. You need no conversation starter or door opener for the gospel other than being the colleague who stays in an attitude of godly gratitude at work.

Colossians 2:6-7 encourages us to continue in our faith as we started in it: "rooted and built up in him and firm in your faith just as you were taught, and overflowing with thankfulness." Our spiritual growth and sanctification should also be with a pouring out of thanksgiving. It's not by our own striving that we become mature in the faith, but rather by God's process of growing us: His wisdom and growth in, and our thanksgiving out. Every mark of spiritual maturity in ourselves should be acknowledged in thanksgiving, rather than causing us to become proud or arrogant because of it.

Our service and gifts to God and to others should also be dripping with thanksgiving as the *charis* lens works. So often, it's our Christian service and giving of ourselves that dries us up spiritually. We can be so excited to give and serve that we busy ourselves with God's work without partaking of His grace in our lives. Service becomes striving, and the sacred things of our loving God become duty. Or we ignore the call to service and sit on the sidelines, allowing others to do all the work and reap the reward. Just like barbecue sauce can revive a tough and dry piece of beef, a dry life can be made rich again with abundant thanksgiving.

Paul describes how we're to serve so that we don't dry up. Read his words carefully:

And God is able to make all grace overflow to you so that because you have enough of everything in every way at all times, you will overflow in every good work. Just as it is written, "He has scattered widely, he has given to the poor; his righteousness remains forever." Now God who provides seed for the sower and bread for food will provide and multiply your supply of seed and will cause the harvest of your righteousness to grow. You will be enriched in every way so that you may be generous on every occasion, which is producing through us thanksgiving to God, because the service of this ministry is not only providing for the needs of the saints but is also overflowing with many thanks to God. Through the evidence of this service they will glorify God because of your obedience to your confession in the gospel of Christ and the generosity of your sharing with them and with everyone. And in their prayers on your behalf they long for you because of the extraordinary grace God has shown to you. Thanks be to God for his indescribable gift! (2 Corinthians 9:8-15)

Notice the language of abundance in the passage. God's grace overflows to us so that we'll overflow in every good work. God's overflowing grace provides us with everything in every way at all times. God provides our seed *and* multiplies it *and* causes our harvest of righteousness to grow. We're enriched in every way so we can be generous on every occasion. This abundance of God's grace and life exercised in us through giving and service will then produce an overflowing of our thanks and worship to God. This is the abundant life — and out of this life (rather than from striving), our gifts and service can be exercised.

So we see how thanksgiving should be poured over prayer and supplication, our words and deeds, our personal sanctification, and our giving and service to the Lord. A more thorough study of thanksgiving would yield many other circumstances in which we're encouraged to give thanks. Too often we think of thanksgiving as a fine wine to be paired with spiritual delicacies on special occasions, particularly when we identify such a large spot of God's grace in our lives that cannot be ignored. But God's grace, being constantly lavished in our lives, needs a pairing that's much more common, though every bit as pleasing. So whether you think of thanksgiving as barbecue sauce, steak sauce, chili sauce, ketchup, or salsa, carry it with you throughout the day. And whatever you do, marinate it, bake it, dip it, and douse it in thanksgiving.

Selah

Let the name of God be praised forever and ever, for wisdom and power belong to him.

He changes times and seasons, deposing some kings and establishing others.

He gives wisdom to the wise; he imparts knowledge to those with understanding; he reveals deep and hidden things.

He knows what is in the darkness, and light resides with him. (Daniel 2:20-2)

O Lord, my Rock and my Redeemer, Greatest treasure of my longing soul, My God, like You there is no other.

True delight is found in You alone—Your grace, a well too deep to fathom, Your love exceeds the heavens' reach, Your truth, a fount of perfect wisdom, My highest good and my unending need.

O Lord, my Rock and my Redeemer, Strong defender of my weary heart, My sword to fight the cruel deceiver, And my shield against his hateful darts, My song when enemies surround me, My hope when tides of sorrow rise, My joy when trials are abounding, Your faithfulness, my refuge in the night.

O Lord, my Rock and my Redeemer, Gracious Savior of my ruined life, My guilt and cross laid on Your shoulders.

In my place You suffered bled and died, You rose, the grave and death are conquered, You broke my bonds of sin and shame.

O Lord, my Rock and my Redeemer, May all my days bring glory to Your Name. (Nathan Stiff)

When Thanksgiving Is Not Worship

There are two instances when thanksgiving is not worship. One instance is when we're truly grateful to God for something He has given us, but are focused on the object. This isn't necessarily a bad thing, though it may sound bad. Imagine your Christmas gift to a favorite four-year-old child. On opening the gift, the child may not immediately write a two-page thank you letter full of glowing endorsements of your character. But you see the child's eyes light up as she unwraps the gift. She jumps up and down and yells, "Thank you, thank you," then runs out of the room to play with the toy. The short expression of gratitude combined with the thrill of joy on the child's face is all the gratitude the benevolent giver needs to warm the heart.

When the Lord is good to provide anything for us, we should come before Him in gratitude. This is why Paul says in 1 Timothy 4:3 that God created food to be received with thanksgiving, then goes on to state, "For every creation of God is good and no food is to be rejected if it is received with thanksgiving" (4:4). That's why we thank our Jehovah Jireh for providing food for us before each meal (we say "grace" or "thanks" —*charis* includes both meanings). We must be careful that this doesn't become a mindless ritual for us, as can happen with anything we do three times daily. But neither must we enter into the praise of His moral perfection every time we sit down to eat. If we're truly grateful for the food we're ready to eat, and we thank God for that food, that's proper gratitude without worship.

Similarly, when we thank the Lord for answered prayers, one can offer quality gratitude without offering true worship. Keeping a prayer journal is an important part of prayer life so that we can look back on all our prayers that the Lord has answered and give Him both thanks and worship. But the Lord answers so many quick prayers throughout our day, as well as granting so many blessings we didn't ask for, that it would be impossible to truly worship Him for everything He does for us. Sometimes a quick and heartfelt "Thank you, Lord," is sufficient.

But pure thanksgiving for an object or situation shouldn't dominate our prayer lives. It may feel as though it's a substitute for worship, but we shouldn't treat it as such unless it's tied to worship in acknowledging the goodness of the Giver. Both flow out of the overflowing abundance of the heart. Both are offered in submission, humility, and dependence. But this type of thanksgiving is focused on the object with a spirit that acknowledges God as the Giver, whereas worship focuses on the Giver and His glorious perfection.

The other instance where giving thanks is not worship is when we focus on the object only, ignoring God as the Giver. Of course, this isn't truly thanksgiving at all, but it may feel as though it is. Millions of Americans celebrate Thanksgiving as a holiday, not knowing to whom they're giving thanks. They like the fact that there's a feast on the table, but they don't give thanks to God. They're like the individuals in Romans 1 who failed to glorify God or give Him thanks (1:21)—perhaps giving thanks to their "lucky stars," good fortune, or chance.

A more obviously sinister attitude may be that of the persons described in James 4:3, who ask so that they can fulfill their passions. These people are happy when they receive things and may also thank their lucky stars before they indulge in satisfaction of the flesh. Think of the businessman who gets a bonus and immediately buys a boat in contrast to the man who immediately brings a joyful money offering to the Lord. Both are happy to have the extra money and feel like they're grateful, but the focus is different. Maybe a woman goes to eat with some friends and has a wonderful time. She can be "thankful" for friends as an evidence of her popularity or as self-affirmation, or she can thank God for His provision of friends in her life.

The distinction between worship and thanksgiving is a crucial one. Gratitude to God for things He provides for us is not only important, it's also beautiful. It's the overflow of God's grace to us in our lives that we send back to Him in thanks. In a wonderful way, it's a childlike part of our walk with the Lord. But like a child, we can be so focused on the "stuff" we receive from the Lord that we forget about His incredible majesty. In a strange twist, what feels like thanksgiving can actually be egocentrism if we bask in the gift and ignore the Giver. The same attitude in a romantic relationship might make us wonder if our counterpart loved us only for what we gave them. Would that love dry up when the gifts dried up? Wouldn't it be nice to be loved for who we are rather than what we do for them?

Of course, God understands our frailty, and He has no need of our worship for His glory to be preeminent. But it's our privilege as His children to see not only His gifts to us but also the eternal glory of His Godhead. When we can look beyond the gift and be enthralled with the Giver much more than the gift, that's true worship.

When Thanksgiving Is Worship

This is not at all to promote asceticism—extreme self-discipline and avoiding all indulgence. Paul warned against that in Colossians 2. We can enjoy the things God provides for us and be grateful for them even when we don't stop to worship. A maturing Christian, however, will find ways to worship *through* thanksgiving. In this way, we see thanksgiving and worship intersect, just as we find throughout the pages of Scripture.

Here's a key verse for worshiping through thanksgiving:

> *All generous giving and every perfect gift is from above, coming down from the Father of lights, with whom there is no variation or the slightest hint of change.* (James 1:17)

When the Lord gives something to us, His giving is generous and the gift is perfect. This is cause for our thanksgiving for the gift. Then with gratitude, we look up from the gift to the Giver to see His generosity and perfect provision. This leads us to worship His attributes more than His gift. Inspired by the teaching in James 1:17, this would mean worshiping His immutability and eternality.

The vast majority of exhortations and examples of thanksgiving in the Scriptures are worshipful thanksgiving. You won't find passages there that say things like, "Give thanks to the Lord for giving you a good day," or, "Come before the Lord with thanksgiving for your job promotion." Rather we find, "Give thanks to the Lord for He is good, and His loyal love endures" (Psalm 118:1), and, "Enter his gates with thanksgiving, and his courts with praise! Give him thanks! Praise his name! For the LORD is good. His loyal love endures, and he is faithful through all generations" (Psalm 100:4-5).

You'll find a strong pattern in the Scriptures that worship through thanksgiving exalts God's goodness and love. That is typically where my heart goes in worshipful thanksgiving. However, we can be thankful for all of God's attributes (even His wrath toward sin) as we observe His attributes demonstrated in our daily lives.

Here are other characteristics of God worshiped through thanksgiving in the Scriptures:

His holiness (Psalm 30:4; 97:12);

His nearness (Psalm 75:1);

His mercy (1 Chronicles 16:41);

His righteousness (Psalm 119:62);

His faithfulness (Psalm 100:5).

All His attributes should cause us not only to worship Him but also to give Him thanks. If God lacked one of His attributes, He wouldn't be possess moral perfection, and He would be somewhere on the spectrum between an evil genius and a jolly old man upstairs. With a God like that, we would not fare well.

We directly benefit from God's mercy, love, holiness, and righteousness *every day*—in so many ways beyond what we can see or even imagine. Just as His character is more vast than the expanse of the entire universe, so is the way in which His character impacts us. We're too feeble and frail to spiritually comprehend all His many benefits for us according to His perfect character. We can see only what's in front of us, and only by the illumination of the Holy Spirit. But if we look for the nuances of His character in the happenings of our daily lives, searching out the riches of His grace in His kindness toward us, we'll overflow with thanksgiving. Paul doesn't pray that the Ephesian believers might just generically know the love of Christ, but he prays that they might know the width, length, height, and depth of Christ's love.

It's the full measure of His character in His dealings with us that will expand the scope of our thankfulness to Him. In light of this, the bounty of physical and spiritual gifts that He showers on us will then be seen in the context of His glory, which will thrill us more than the generous and perfect gifts He has given us. Therefore we're told, "Since we're receiving an unshakeable kingdom, let us give thanks, and through this let us offer worship pleasing to God in devotion and awe" (Hebrews 12:28).

To be included in God's final plan for the end of the ages is an incredible thing! What have you or I done to merit such favor? Absolutely nothing! This is God's grace toward us, otherwise known as His unmerited favor. So then, using the *charis* lens, God's grace poured into our lives should result in thanksgiving flowing out of our hearts and mouths. Too many times, we ponder His grace toward us and stop at the feeling of amazement. *We must go on to give thanks.* Then, according this passage, we ought to offer worship to God through our thanksgiving in devotion and awe.

If your time in the Word feels dry and monochromatic, it may be because you're stopping at reading and studying. Even pondering doesn't return the light of God's grace shone into our lives. Read and study, ponder, give thanks, worship.

Finally, when thanksgiving is worship, it's the most relational aspect of our worship toward God. Most aspects of worship focus on God as our Sovereign, a deity who's far beyond our grasp of knowledge or practice. Even His love for us, when we properly worship Him, forces us to acknowledge our unworthiness and unloveliness. But worship through thanksgiving helps us relate to God as our Abba Father, and as Jehovah Jireh, our Provider.

Thanksgiving emanates from receiving tangible expressions of God's grace in our lives. It's from tasting and seeing that the Lord is good. The more we worship God through thanksgiving, the more we notice His goodness toward us. It's a blessed cycle that makes God feel as near to us as He is. It becomes a constant reminder of His attributes that helps us move on from theoretical worship. We're shown firsthand how God is our beneficent Provider, and we are His cared-for children. It erases doubt and anxiety that God may fail to provide or care for us.

So let's follow the example of David as He says:

I will give you thanks with all my heart; before the heavenly assembly I will sing praises to you. I will bow down toward your holy temple, and give thanks to your name, because of your loyal love and faithfulness, for you have exalted your promise above the entire sky. (Psalm 138:1-2)

Study Questions

1. The charis lens is interrupted when we don't recognize God's grace, or when we don't accept that grace. In which areas of your life can you more clearly recognize God's grace, so that you can "in everything give thanks"?

2. How are worship and thanksgiving similar? How are they different?

3. Read 2 Corinthians 4:15-16. What is one of the results of the charis lens (grace in, and thanksgiving out)?

Chapter 12
The Palette: Practical Practice in Worshipping God

I'll never forget watching the NBA finals in 1999 between the New York Knicks and the San Antonio Spurs. During a timeout, a microphone transmitted the coach of the Knicks adamantly telling his team, "Get a stop, and then a score. A stop, then a score. Stop and score." I'm sure his team would have agreed that this is a good game plan. If only I could be paid millions of dollars to tell a basketball team, "If you score more points than your opponent, we'll win this game." However, it's the practical game plan that will help us score more points than our opponent.

Worship is much the same way. While we would all agree that worshiping God every day in our conversation and prayers is important, we would probably also agree that it's not as easy as just having a desire to worship God.

So where do we start in our daily worship of God? Let's explore some ways that can turn this desire into a practical reality.

Selah——The Pause

The writers of the Psalms frequently wrote the musical term *selah* into their compositions. Although the exact meaning of the term doesn't have a consensus definition, it's thought that *selah* is a pause or interlude intended to bring the listener into reflection.

With so many things constantly pulling us in every direction and demanding our attention, we must ensure that we aren't distracted when we approach the throne room in worship. Many people have told me their best prayer times are in the car on their commute to work; it's when they're least distracted. Although I also like to worship on the commute, I smile to myself when I hear this. If hurtling down a highway in two tons of metal at a hundred feet per second constitutes the most meditative part of our day, there may be a problem with our society.

God's glory deserves more than our distracted affections. Until we're impressed by the weight of His glory to the point of pausing our day to offer praise, our words of worship will be fabricated. God warns us that He won't share His glory with another. I cannot therefore give less mental energy to God's splendor than I do to balancing my bank account. I cannot give less emotional energy to Him than I give my frustrating day at work. I cannot give less spiritual energy to Him than I do to being busy in His service. God must consume my energies and dominate my affections, not compete with them.

King David understood this. In 2 Samuel 7, after God makes His covenant with David and His descendants, David doesn't merely say, "Oh, praise God," then go about his business. His actual response serves as a great template for how we should stop to worship the Lord:

> King David went in, sat before the Lord, and said, "Who am I, O Lord God, and what is my family, that you should have brought me to this point? And you didn't stop there, O Lord God! You have also spoken about the future of your servant's family. Is this your usual way of dealing with men, O Lord God? What more can David say to you? You have given your servant special recognition, O Lord God! For the sake of your promise and according to your purpose you have done this great thing in order to reveal it to your servant. Therefore you are great, O Lord God, for there is none like you! There is no God besides you! What we have heard is true! Who is like your people, Israel, a unique nation on the

earth? Their God went to claim a nation for himself and to make a name for himself! You did great and awesome acts for your land, before your people whom you delivered for yourself from the Egyptian empire and its gods. You made Israel your very own people for all time. You, O Lord, became their God. So now, O Lord God, make this promise you have made about your servant and his family a permanent reality. Do as you promised, so you may gain lasting fame, as people say, 'The Lord of hosts is God over Israel!' The dynasty of your servant David will be established before you, for you, O Lord of hosts, the God of Israel, have told your servant, 'I will build you a dynastic house.' That is why your servant has had the courage to pray this prayer to you. Now, O sovereign Lord, you are the true God! May your words prove to be true! You have made this good promise to your servant! Now be willing to bless your servant's dynasty so that it may stand permanently before you, for you, O sovereign Lord, have spoken. By your blessing may your servant's dynasty be blessed on into the future!" (2 Samuel 7:18-29)

David first stopped and sat before the Lord. Being a king, he probably had other things he could have been doing besides sitting before the Lord. He saw the value of stopping to praise and thank God for His faithfulness. Furthermore, in the quietness of his chamber, he used his intellectual, emotional, and spiritual energies to compose a worshipful prayer that was neither generic nor hurried.

Stopping to worship is more than just a spiritual discipline for health and growth. It's where God meets us and reveals Himself to us. He tells us,

Stop your striving and recognize that I am God! I will be exalted over the nations! I will be exalted over the earth! (Psalm 46:10)

Our faith may be small, and our worship life smaller, if we aren't in the habit of stopping and being still. This could mean getting alone with God in creation, hitting our knees in the bedroom, or even taking a few extra minutes in the bathroom. God will meet with us and reveal Himself to us anywhere, if we stop and give him our full attention.

Read Scripture

Once we've stopped, Scripture is where we start. We cannot worship God if we don't know Him as He reveals Himself to us in Scripture. Every verse of Scripture is a treasure of wisdom that tells us something about God. Even the Bible's stories about people and its commentaries on mankind will tell us about God's relationship to us.

Our worship of God shouldn't stop at reading about Him, as it often does. When we read about one of His attributes, or something that He does, let's stop to reflect and praise Him for this. Read Scripture with the intent to pray it back to Him in worship.

For instance, we should stop and worship when we read these words of Jesus:

> *Take my yoke on you and learn from me, because I am gentle and humble in heart, and you will find rest for your souls.* (Matthew 11:29)

Come before the Lord's throne and praise Him that, although He's the Sovereign of the universe, Jesus is still approachable. He wants us to partake in His Spirit. He's humble and gentle. In the entire cosmos, only He is able to give us rest for our souls. And He wants us to find it. Praise the Lord!

You can study the Word deeply to find more insight, or you can worship from simple reading. You can compose your own song of worship to the Lord, or you can use God's own words to praise Him.

Of course, if we wish to build a lifestyle of worship that constantly exalts God, we must take God's Word about Himself with us and integrate it into our lives. We do that through memorization and meditation. The psalmist wrote of the value of these in worship:

> *In my heart I store up your words, so I might not sin against you. You deserve praise, O LORD! Teach me your statutes! With my lips I proclaim all the regulations you have revealed. I rejoice in the lifestyle prescribed by your rules as if they were riches of all kinds. I will meditate on your precepts and focus on your behavior.*
> (Psalm 119:11-15)

We make things of God so difficult on ourselves by not memorizing Scripture and meditating on it. People often complain that memorizing Scripture is difficult. No, what's truly difficult is trying to walk worthy of our calling *without* memorizing Scripture. When we read the Word in the morning, how can we possibly expect to remember what we read when we're later assaulted with information and trying situations throughout our day? How are we to fight the spiritual battle if we don't bring our sword with us hour by hour? How are we to worship the Lord continually if His excellence isn't continually churning in our minds?

For God's Word to have its perfect effect in our lives, we must have it memorized. Otherwise, the world affects us twenty-three hours daily while God's Word affects us for only one hour. Which influence will win out in our lives? However, if we only memorize Scripture and don't meditate on it throughout the day so as to engraft it into our lives, the memorization is blunted in its effect; it's a purely technical exercise.

So how do we take the words of Scripture and use them in worship of God? Certainly all Scripture tells us something about God and can therefore be used in worship. But I've found that worshiping God from the pages of Scripture is easier for me if I think of three main areas of worship: who God is, what He has done, and our relationship to Him.

Who Is God?

We sometimes erroneously misconstrue theology—and particularly God's attributes—as only intellectual fodder. But learning God's attributes is essential for knowing Him intimately, drawing closer to Him, and worshiping Him. The more of God's attributes we learn and worship, the more we'll have a complete and complex understanding of Him, moving on from the milk of the Word to the meat.

Think of a hologram versus a normal photograph. Both provide representations of a subject that are fairly realistic. However, with a normal photograph, we're able to see only two-dimensionally. When we look at a picture of someone straight on, we can see the color of their eyes and their height, and we have a rough estimate of their build, but we miss that third dimension that really enables us to know their exact appearance. With a hologram, every curve and nuance is elucidated by the laser. With the three-dimensional replication of appearance, we're able to view a person much more realistically and tell how big their nose is or what kind of haircut they have.

God offers us the knowledge of the riches of His glory in the many pages of Scripture. He could have given us a two-dimensional view of His character by giving us the Bible in tables and charts or memes. Instead, He gives us the holographic description of His character, offering cooperative angles of His personality, different outworkings of His character, visions of His heart and desires, and His future plans for His glory. We study these aspects of Him in the Bible so that we can form a detailed, multidimensional image of Him to glorify Him. Michelangelo's challenge for himself was that every block of stone has a statue inside it, and the sculptor's task was to discover it. It's the challenge of the Christian to read every page of Scripture with the desire to discover the details of God's character inside those pages. Then we can worship God in detail.

A. W. Tozer said, "What comes into our minds when we think about God is the most important thing about us." This is absolutely true. The title of "God" is merely an office. Billions of people on this earth would say, "I believe in God," and yet many of them will not be in heaven. Christ says that even many of those who name His name aren't true believers and will not be in heaven (Matthew 7:21). The difference is in what we believe about God and about who He is.

Even a well-meaning individual who thinks he's a Christian will set up a false god to worship if his doctrine isn't biblical. For instance, one might say that God created everything, is sovereign, made the past and controls the future, is able to do miraculous things, is eternal, and governs the affairs of man. So far so good, right? But then they might say that God is more of an idea than a being, that there's no hell, and that Jesus was merely a good man and a good prophet. This "God" being described is likely to be the false god of chance. We could make similar scenarios for humanism, cult gods, hedonism, or any other thing that people worship. The living God of the Bible is unique, and we must know His attributes to keep us from false worship.

To learn God's attributes, read the Scriptures and pause to ask, *What does this passage tell me about God?* This is a beautiful way to make the Scriptures come alive! Every page from Genesis to Revelation tells us something about God. Write those things down as the Lord reveals them to you. In theology, we're a bit too fascinated with fifty-cent words such as *immutability* and *transcendence*. These are good terms, but you don't have to pen your discoveries in large words. Write the passage's revelation in full sentences or even paragraphs. Then worship God. Tell Him what you've learned about Him and how it humbles you. Praise Him for His perfection of character. Ask Him to show you more.

For example, in 1 Kings 19 we're given the account of Elijah after

God defeats the prophets of Baal on Mount Carmel. Jezebel has just issued a determined death threat against Elijah, and Elijah flees into the wilderness. He cries out to God in desperation and self-pity, and the Lord answers him.

The LORD said, "Go out and stand on the mountain before the LORD. Look, the LORD is ready to pass by." A very powerful wind went before the LORD, digging into the mountain and causing landslides, but the LORD was not in the wind. After the windstorm there was an earthquake, but the LORD was not in the earthquake. After the earthquake, there was a fire, but the LORD was not in the fire. After the fire, there was a soft whisper. When Elijah heard it, he covered his face with his robe and went out and stood at the entrance to the cave. All of a sudden a voice asked him, "Why are you here, Elijah?" (1 Kings 19:11-13)

From this passage, we see many things about God:

He's willing to show Himself to those in need.
He controls the most powerful aspects of nature.
His voice is sometimes heard in quietness and stillness.
His presence is awe-inspiring.
He's interested in our affairs.
He doesn't want us to wallow in self-pity.
He has a plan and mission for us.

You may have drawn out additional characteristics of God from the passage, but this list gives us plenty to worship Him for. Take your list of God's characteristics from the passage and worship Him for it in prayer.

For example:

> Lord, You control the most powerful forces of nature and are mighty over all. Yet, You care for me enough to show Yourself to me in a way that I can comprehend. Why do You care so much about me when I have rebelled against You and feel that I deserve better than Your loving hand has given me? The depths of Your love and mercy are beyond my comprehension! Yet You do not let me wallow in the misery of my own rebellion and self-pity, but You gently reprove me, as my loving Father, when I'm out of fellowship with You, so that Your holy image will be more clearly seen in my life.

The names God calls Himself by in the Bible also reveal much to us about His character. Throughout the Bible we're given insight into people's character through their names. Notable examples include Jacob (Israel), Nabal, and Naomi (Mara). Names are important to God, who equates His own name with His glory: "I am the LORD! That is my name! I will not share my glory with anyone else, or the praise due me with idols" (Isaiah 42:8). We also know that there are actions that the Lord takes "for His name's sake" (Psalms 31:3; 106:8; Ezekiel 20:44; Isaiah 48:9-11).

Since the Lord regards His name with such gravity, so should we. His many names give us plenty of material for worship. So when we study the Bible (especially the Old Testament), we should make sure that we understand the particular name of God being used, since it's always important and can be used to worship Him. When we sit down to eat, we can praise our Jehovah Jireh ("the LORD will provide"). When we recover from an illness, we can praise Jehovah Rapha ("the LORD who heals"). When we see the sovereign workings of God in our lives, we can praise El Shaddai ("God Almighty").

God loves us so much that He calls us by name. Jesus says that He calls His own sheep by name and leads them out (John 10:3). God tells Israel that He'll protect them and call them by name because they're His (Isaiah 43:1). As part of our new identity, God even gives us new names, so we go from being "unloved" to "loved," from "Not My people" to "My people and sons of the living God" (Romans 9:25-26). God sees our names as important in His relationship with us, so we should view His names as important in our relationship with Him.

Because of the importance of God's name, we should never even come close to taking God's name in vain. If honoring His name is the worship that He desires, taking His name in vain places us in a precarious position of scorn for our loving Father and great God. In biblical times, there was such awe and respect for God that the entirety of His name was not even spoken aloud. But today we flippantly say things like "Good Lord," "Sweet baby Jesus," "Oh God" (or OMG), or "Pah-RAISE the LAWWRD," all perhaps in response to a restaurant serving our favorite variety of tacos. Saying such things in such a manner is an inexcusable travesty for God's people. The third commandment in Exodus 20 carries a dire warning for transgression: "For the Lord will not hold guiltless anyone who takes His name in vain."

God's attributes and character are absolutely everything in the Christian faith. The sustaining of the created world is dependent on them. Our salvation—initial, present, and future—is dependent on them. We draw breath because of them. Our spiritual inheritance flows from them. And while none of these things are dependent on our knowledge of them, it's only by knowing what God reveals about Himself that we can truly understand the world, mankind, the past, the future (into eternity), and our purpose in life. When we seek to know the One who holds in His hands all things, all wisdom, and all power, we'll never run out of things to worship Him for.

Selah

This is what the LORD, Israel's king, says, their protector, the LORD who commands armies:

"I am the first and I am the last, there is no God but me.

Who is like me? Let him make his claim!

Let him announce it and explain it to me—since I established an ancient people—let them announce future events!

Don't panic! Don't be afraid! Did I not tell you beforehand and decree it?

You are my witnesses! Is there any God but me? There is no other sheltering rock; I know of none.
(Isaiah 44:6-8)

The LORD's shout bends the large trees and strips the leaves from the forests.

Everyone in his temple says, "Majestic!"

The LORD sits enthroned over the engulfing waters, the LORD sits enthroned as the eternal king.

The LORD gives his people strength; the LORD grants his people security. (Psalm 29:9-11)

What Has God Done?

Remembrance is a key concept in our worship of God. Throughout the Scriptures, God exhorts those who have a relationship with Him to remember what He has done. We're commanded to remember God's interventions when we're in distress (Psalm 77:9-11), when we're celebrating (1 Chronicles 16:12), and when we're afraid (Deuteronomy 7:17-19). In remembrance, we're to teach our children what God has done (Deuteronomy 6:20-23), and tell others of His great deeds (Joshua 4:21-24). We're to remember his deeds in our thankfulness (Psalm 9:1) and in many more circumstances throughout the Scripture.

Not remembering was the downfall for the children of Israel when they complained in the wilderness, thinking that they had it good in Egypt and that God brought them into the wilderness only to kill them. Failure to remember caused Israel's spies to give a bad report and to counsel against entering the land of Canaan, causing further wandering in the desert. It was also why Jonah became bitter at God when He spared Nineveh.

Remembering God's interventions and blessings in our lives is crucially important. We receive blessing at His hand, then too often forget about His goodness a day later when trials come.

Remembrance is a nice way to worship God through conversation. Those of us who lack eloquence may not always feel comfortable describing God's attributes to unbelievers in conversation. Rarely do we get asked by a secular colleague at work, "What attribute of God are you dwelling on today?" But how many times a day are we asked, "How are you?" or "What's going on?" These questions are open invitations to brag on the Lord and report the great things that He has done for us:

"I'm up to my ears in work, but the Lord has given me a real peace about it."

"I messed up the other day, but the Lord intervened for me."

"The Lord is blessing me with green pastures and still waters in my soul!"

"Life is rough right now, but the Lord is giving me a sense of His loving presence."

Psalm 136 is a one of many examples in the Bible of worship through remembrance. It's originally meant to be sung antiphonally, with one party singing the first part of each verse (praising God for

His mighty acts) and the other party singing the second part (responding with worship of God's character: "For His loyal love endures").

Also consider the paralyzed man in Luke 5 and the lame man in Acts 3. Both men, when miraculously healed, immediately worshiped God. The paralyzed man was the newest forgiven sinner on the planet, and there's no indication that the lame man was a believer at the time of his healing, so I doubt they were worshiping and glorifying God for some deep theological concept. More likely, they were simply praising Him for His intervention in their lives. Such a simple praise doesn't need to be much more than a testimony, but it gives honor to whom honor is due.

Earlier we discussed how worship can be an antidote for depression and anxiety. Worshiping God's intervention in our lives reminds us that He loves us, is sovereign, and is concerned with our affairs. David mentions the value of remembering God's works as a weapon against depression and anxiety in Psalm 143. He speaks of his overwhelmed and distressed heart, then states,

> *I recall the old days; I meditate on all you have done; I reflect on your accomplishments.* (143:5)

The wonderful thing about this is that we can worship God by relating His actions to His character. All God's actions flow from His attributes. His consistency of character guarantees that He'll never act against His attributes. This isn't so with us. Certainly not by nature, but by practice, most people would say they're an individual of good will. Most of the times when I give someone a gift, it's because I have some amount of benevolence toward them. But there are times when I give gifts out of ulterior motives that don't match with the general perception of my good-willed character. God, however, is consistent in His sinless perfection, so all His actions are consistent with all of His character. This enables us to worship His character by recounting what He has done for us. We can worship His love and wisdom when

He withholds things that we want that may be harmful to us. We can see His goodness when He gives us things we want. We see His grace mercifully imparted to us when He enables us to forgive someone who has wronged us.

Look for God's hand in your life and praise Him for it. Remember what He has done for you—not just today, but in the last month, year, and decade. Your life is a continuous and ever-lengthening song of praise to the Lord. All you need to do is sing it.

God's Relationship to Us

If you're a believer, your true identity is who you are *in Christ*—nothing more and nothing less. Your identity is not what you do professionally. It's not your strengths and weaknesses. It's your identity in Christ, which is completely based on relationship to God through Christ. This knowledge will help us in all our struggles, and will also help us worship God through His revelation to us in His Word.

Identity is rooted in relationship. When we consider our physical identity, it involves our relationship to our physical family, especially if our family is respected or there are good feelings about them. Recently I was speaking with a high schooler I'd just met, and I asked her to tell me about herself. She told me her name and the name of her father, quickly mentioning his importance to the community as a popular country music artist. Although she didn't do anything to deserve that relationship to her well-known father, she proudly exhibited that relationship as a main part of her identity. Her philosophy on life, her likes and dislikes, and her lifestyle may all change through the years, but her physical relationship to her family will not.

More significant than the physical identity is our spiritual identity. We would have far fewer struggles in life if we found our total identity in being children of our heavenly Father. With this mindset, anxiety melts away because nothing can separate us from the love of God (Romans 8:38-39). Depression is lifted because God treasures us as His children (1 John 3:1). The shackles of besetting sin can be broken because our old man has died with Christ and our new man has been resurrected with Him (Romans 6:5-12). Unfortunately, we often live as though our identity comes from our vocation, personalities, likes and dislikes, or other relatively insignificant things.

Because we've done nothing to merit our identity in Christ, we can take joy in adoring God because of it. All through the pages of Scripture, God makes sure we know that we're His children. As His children, we're told that He loves us. We can worship Him for this whenever we feel alone or unloved. We're told that He disciplines us as children (Hebrews 12:6-7). We can worship Him for this when we sin and experience sin's consequences. We have constant access to the throne of God (Hebrews 4:16), who is both our sovereign King and our Father. This should make us worship every time we pray. We've been qualified by the Father to share in the inheritance of the saints (Colossians 1:12). We've received the Spirit of adoption so we can be co-heirs with Christ (Romans 8:15,17). He exchanged our filthy rags of sin and self-righteousness for garments of salvation and robes of righteousness (Isaiah 61:10). The Holy Spirit indwells us at the time of our salvation and subsequently works to seal us, assure us of salvation, guide us, gift us, and produce fruit in us (Ephesians 1:13; Romans 8:16; John 16:13; 1 Corinthians 12; Galatians 5:22-23).

There are so many aspects of God's relationship with us that are worth exploring and worshiping Him for. We discover them in some of the most precious verses in all of Scripture—precious because they give us new identity as God's beloved. Because these verses are fundamental to our faith, they're well known and often glossed over in our Scripture reading without our giving them much thought. They're also celebrated in most of our Christian children's songs. But familiarity should never lead to casualness. While we may already know a plethora of verses that describe our adoption into God's family, I hope there's a fresh wave of delightful awe every time we read about this and realize how blessed we are because of it.

Seasons in our walk with the Lord naturally come and go. There are seasons of zeal, seasons of acquiring knowledge, seasons of labor, and seasons of intimacy with the Lord. We especially long for the day when the season of intimacy with the Lord will become permanent. While we're still here on earth, worshiping God for His relationship with us brings us into the awareness of that intimacy. I strongly encourage you to focus on this if you feel that your walk with the Lord lacks intimacy. As you search the Scriptures, you'll be surprised how much the Bible says about God's relationship with us when we look for it for the purpose of worship.

In summary, as we approach the Scriptures seeking to worship God for His perfect character, for things He has done, and for His relationship with us, it becomes difficult to turn the page because of the abundance of praiseworthy text. The Word wasn't given for the purpose of our learning a secret handshake or paying dues to stay in good standing with the Lord. Nor is it to be read primarily as a code of ethics for moral living. It's His revelation to us about Himself, given to bring us into an eternity of fellowship with Him and to give us a head start on worshiping Him. When we approach it in this way, it vanquishes the drudgery of needing to read two chapters of the Bible per day just to be a good Christian. The grayscale approach to the Word becomes colorful, and the monochromatic walk with God becomes lustrous and iridescent. More importantly, we read the Scriptures for the purpose that they were written—to help us become true worshipers of God.

Sing

Singing touches us uniquely. It expresses and transforms our spirit and soul. There's a deep subconscious communication that occurs with singing. We see this in the fact that the most lauded singers are those with whom we make an emotional or spiritual connection. The most popular songs are those that grab our hearts strongly, because the words tell the stories of our souls better than we can.

The drive for connection in singing is so strong that it breaks the paradigm of entertainment. Typically in entertainment, we're drawn to that which we could never do but wish we could: a figure skater's triple flip, a quarterback's 350-passing-yard game, a Rachmaninov piano concerto, or motocross racing. With singing, however, we're drawn to songs we can sing ourselves. There's a reason why operatic arias that employ three octaves of vocal range or vocal renditions of "Flight of the Bumblebee" are not the greatest hits. It's because they don't work themselves into our shower-singing repertoire. The subliminal value of singing is that we connect with our inner being and with those around us.

Worship through singing engages mind, soul, and spirit so that our inner feelings of awe and adoration are thoroughly expressed. The importance of singing is highlighted by the fact that it's mentioned nearly two hundred times in the Bible. Although this is usually in reference to praising the Lord, singing also helps us encourage others in the Lord. As believers, what should our social gatherings look like? Paul tells us:

> *And do not get drunk with wine, which is debauchery, but be filled by the Spirit, speaking to one another in psalms, hymns, and spiritual songs, singing and making music in your hearts to the Lord, always giving thanks to God the Father for each other in the name of our Lord Jesus Christ, and submitting to one another out of reverence for Christ.* (Ephesians 5:18-21)

There are many insights for worshipful singing in this passage. Being loosened by alcohol and being filled with (or controlled by) the Holy Spirit are mutually exclusive, and only one of those states can fashion true worship. The other may spawn singing and emotionalism, but not true worship. The phrase "speaking to one another" implies antiphonal singing; that is, call and response. It's the type of singing mentioned earlier in Psalm 136, used for bringing people together in the worship of the Lord. Our worship of God isn't meant to be purely private with Him, but also conversational with others.

We also see that God is eclectic in His preferred style of worship singing. From these three mentioned types of worship songs, one cannot isolate a single style that's solely pleasing to the Lord. More important is that our worship is Spirit-filled, edifying to one another, heartfelt, full of thanksgiving to God, respectful to one another, and not self-promoting. Worshipful singing should always encourage and edify rather than disgust and divide.

In regard to "worship wars," and bringing unity through worship, Russell Moore writes:

> Maybe we need to reignite the wars, but in a Christian sort of way... What if the young singles complained that the drums are too loud, that they're distracting the senior adults? What if the elderly people complained that the church wasn't paying attention to the new movements in songwriting or musical style? When we seek the well-being of others in worship, it's not just that we cringe through music we hate. As an act of love, this often causes us to appreciate, empathize, and even start to resonate with worship through musical forms we previously never considered.

Though somewhat tongue-in-cheek, this is a modern-day application of Ephesians 5:18-21.

In addition to maintaining the church's unity *in* corporate worship, we must strive for edification of the body *through* corporate worship. This means there's no excuse for the lifeless face in the congregation who justifies not singing because he's worshiping in His soul, or doesn't like the style of music. God declares in Scripture that He wants us to sing; if we valued that desire as highly as we do His other directives, I wonder what difference that would make in our congregational singing, our fellowship times during the week, and our personal quiet times.

Singing also changes the emotion of our soul and status of our spirit. So many times for me, singing a song of worship to the Lord has turned around a bad day at work or with people. When we sing to the Lord and worship His grandeur, His heart communes with ours, and our outlook improves substantially. Such a powerful instrument that brings us into God's throne room and also makes life more beautiful should hardly be used sparingly.

Singing is in fact such a spiritual entity that we're told the angels were singing at the dawn of time. Job 38:7 gives us a glimpse of the heavenly chorale as it speaks of the morning stars singing in chorus, and all the sons of God shouting for joy. We're also told that the angels and elders of heaven will be singing alongside us at the end of all things (Revelation 5:8-9).

David valued singing so much that he was determined to be singing the Lord's praises before the dawn, and he committed to singing God's praises to all foreigners (Psalm 57:7-9). Ethan the Ezrahite's desire was to make the greatness of the Lord known to all generations through singing (Psalm 89:1). Paul and Silas were singing praise to God while imprisoned in Philippi (Acts 16:25). They could have prayed silently so as not to "embarrass the Lord" with their singing voices amid their imprisonment; instead they chose to sing praise. Interestingly, the text specifically notes that the other prisoners were listening to them. They were no doubt encouraged (or perhaps made curious) by the worshipful spirit exhibited by these men despite their suboptimal situation.

We learn in Scripture that singing is to be done not only corporately but also in private and on our beds (Psalms 149:5; 77:6). After all, God is the one who gives us songs in the night (Job 35:10). Singing can implement all the aspects of high quality worship: expression, humility, emotion, truth, community, and intimacy with

God. And singing to the Lord is pleasant (Psalms 135:3; 147:1).

Although singing can transform the spirit and soul in a godly way, it can also be a portal for ungodly transformation. If the music conveys chaos and anger, these will take root in our souls. If the lyrics promote discontentment and lust, you'll probably struggle with these sins. Even in some of our church songs, the lyrics may be more likely to rid your mind of the Holy Spirit than to fill it. Be careful with the lyrics you listen to and sing.

Singing is one of God's greatest gifts to us, designed by Him to elevate our spirits and to allow beautiful communion with Him. The Lord has gifted us with voices capable of singing to Him as an instrument to bring us into worship. We should make frequent use of this gift, and praise God with spirit, soul, and voice.

Selah

The LORD is great and certainly worthy of praise!

No one can fathom his greatness!

One generation will praise your deeds to another, and tell about your mighty acts!

I will focus on your honor and majestic splendor, and your amazing deeds!

They will proclaim the power of your awesome acts!

I will declare your great deeds!

They will talk about the fame of your great kindness, and sing about your justice.

The LORD is merciful and compassionate; he is patient and demonstrates great loyal love.

The LORD is good to all, and has compassion on all he has made. (Psalm 145:3-9)

Write Worship

Charles Wesley is generally regarded as the most influential hymnwriter in the last millennium. He was raised in church and had intense biblical training from a young age at the hands of his godly parents. However, he realized later in life that his faith in Christ wasn't genuine. At the age of thirty, he trusted Christ as his personal Savior. He opened his Bible to Psalm 40:3 and read, "He hath put a new song in my mouth; many will see and fear and will trust in the Lord." Shortly thereafter, he penned the lyrics to "And Can It Be?"

That hymn includes these words:

Long my imprisoned spirit lay
Fast bound in sin and nature's night;
Thine eye diffused a quick'ning ray —
I woke, the dungeon flamed with light;
My chains fell off, my heart was free,
I rose, went forth, and followed Thee.

Hymnwriting was more for Charles Wesley than a way to publish and make money. It was more than coining material that Christians of his day needed. It was his own worship to the Lord. It was also a declaration of biblical theology that would lead people into worship of God for His revealed attributes. Charles Wesley didn't have the gift of teaching from the pulpit that his brother John had. But Charles wrote some of the most beautiful songs of worship and theology that we have, writing them as his love letters to the Lord. He wrote, "Keep us little and unknown, prized and loved by God alone."

Love letters are inexplicably wonderful. Years after our wedding, Katherine's letters to me still make me deeply happy. While I love reading her letters, I enjoy equally writing letters to her. This is because I've found that my verbalized affection for her falls terribly short of my feelings for her. I usually get stuck with "I love you more than I can express," or "You mean so much to me." I'm not exceptionally creative in the moment. But when I write letters to her, I'm able to express a much deeper and comprehensive emotion. I even find myself falling more and more in love with her as I write, which fuels an even more passionate expression of my love and commitment. My letters aren't even close to quality prose or poetry, but I don't care, and neither does Katherine. Especially in the mundaneness of everyday life, a love letter rekindles the expression of love for her in my own heart and ensures her that she's not taken for granted.

Our relationship with God is similar. Few of us have tongues skilled enough to instantaneously worship God the way our hearts and spirit desire—and that's okay! Write your worship of God, then pray or sing it to Him. It doesn't have to be skilled. If you get stuck, use what the Holy Spirit showed you from your time in the Word and in prayer. Write about God's intervention in your life as Charles Wesley did in writing *And Can It Be* right after he was saved.

It may be discouraging to attempt to worship God in prayer or conversation when others are around us. A tongue-tied and shallow prayer is often the result (I speak from experience). Writing worship releases the pressure of spontaneity, but it also prepares us with thought and material for future spontaneous worship. The extra time and thought also allows us to meditate on Scripture and allows the Holy Spirit to impress all the beautiful and more subtle shades of God's glory upon us. You'll plunge into a deeper worship as you write your love letters to God.

If appropriate, pledge to yourself that your writings will be for His ears only, and that you won't seek to capitalize on them. This will allow you to write deeper and more honestly, without the pressure of turning out something publishable. The flesh is deceitful—always looking for an opportunity to exalt itself. If you experience intimate worship from something you wrote for God, your flesh may tempt you to share this with the world—which could well become an opportunity to distract you away from the riches of God's presence, and instead tempt you toward the imaginations and worship of self-notoriety or money.

As you write, enter into God's presence, into the beauty of His holiness. Marvel at His goodness. Commune with the good Shepherd, praising His watchful care of you. Savor your immersion into the wonders of His attributes.

Take your time writing each line to the King of kings. Fall to your knees in awe that you can enter into a romance with the Sovereign of the universe, and write your love letter of worship.

Enjoy Creation

In my clinic, I sometimes see patients who've had surgery performed by other surgeons. You can tell a lot about a surgeon just by looking at their work. I may see evidence of a sloppy surgery, leading me to think that the surgeon didn't care or was relatively unskilled. I may see evidence of a complication during the surgery, but then see how beautifully that complication was taken care of, and I conclude that it was a tough surgery performed by a good surgeon. My favorite, of course, is when I see a pristine surgery where no shortcuts were taken and each step was textbook perfect. That's the work of a meticulous surgeon.

Similarly, God's work in creation tells us much about Him. Once you get beyond the concrete jungle of the city and find some flora and fauna, you'll realize that creation really does declare God's handiwork. We need only watch and listen. Watch a flock of geese migrate. How do they know where to go and when? What is wind, and how can seemingly "nothing" be so forceful or so pleasant? How do bats know to make and use a vortex to get out of a cave, and how do they create a vortex without hitting each other? You can of course look up the answers in a textbook, but do that only after you've watched and wondered. The design is incredible.

Nature gives us plenty of worshipful material for praising the sovereign Creator. Look at the beautiful trees, grass, and clouds in the sky, and worship God for His aesthetic creativity in the vastness of creation. Each cloud, flower, and tree is so different from another, and absolutely gorgeous in its own way. The Lord is gracious to us to be so creative for our pleasure and enjoyment. He could have made creation to be only functional—one type of grass for animals to eat, one type of cloud for rain, one type of tree for oxygen creation and shade.

God is also orderly. Consider the DNA codes that give blueprints for life. There's so much consistency in DNA codes throughout all types of life. Although science hasn't completely elucidated it, there's a complex order to the laws of genetic coding, namely replication (where DNA reproduces itself), transcription (where copies of RNA are made from the DNA template), and translation (where the RNA copies are used to make proteins). This precise and complex order gives way to the incredible creativity and diversity of life. The complexity is such that there are even components of the system designed to search for errors in the code, excise them, and rebuild the strand of DNA or RNA. What's incredible is that this process has significant variation among classes of organisms, so that all achieve a similar result: creation of proteins that build, signal, degrade, transport, replicate, and repair within the organism. By signals and tags, those proteins know exactly where to go and what to do upon being manufactured.

On the opposite end of the size spectrum, consider the organization of the stars, galaxies, and all the universe. If Earth were just a few percentage points closer or further from the sun (which could easily happen if the earth were to speed up or slow down), our planet would be uninhabitable. Think also about the predictability of the constellations, eclipses, and comets.

Or consider the tight adherence of nature to laws of physics and mathematics. There are so many laws of physics and mathematics that perfectly describe what's happening in nature. And tomorrow, those same laws will hold true. Yet these laws are what give rise to the awesomeness of a supernova, the creative storytelling of the constellations, and the beauty of a fiery sunset.

God's creativity and organization are just a few of the things that creation leads us to worship Him for. We can bow before His power in an intense thunderstorm that we know He controls. We can thank Him for His peace on a warm, breezy spring day in a grass-filled meadow (meditate on Psalm 23). We can praise His faithfulness to His promises when we see His provision for His creation through plants and animals.

In Romans 1, Paul writes about people rejecting God despite the overwhelming detail of His attributes in creation. Allow me to retool verses 20, 21, and 25 from that passage to describe the worshiping believer's response to God's creation:

> Since the creation of the world, God's invisible attributes—His eternal power and divine nature—are clearly seen, because they're understood through what has been made. So we glorify Him as God and give Him thanks. We acknowledge the truth of God, and we worship and serve the Creator, who is blessed forever! Amen.

Study Questions

1. Read 1 Kings 19:11-13. What does this passage teach us about the importance of stopping to listen for God?

2. Read Psalm 150. How are we to worship? When are we to worship? Who is to worship? Where are we to worship?

Chapter 13
Everyday Worship

A fact of life is that I'm not a bodybuilding hulk of a man. I could identify in my mind as a bodybuilder. I could falsely tell people I'm six-foot-three and 240 pounds of solid muscle. I could even take on some of the habits of a bodybuilder—drinking protein shakes, and each day eating 10,000 calories and exercising at the gym, but that wouldn't necessarily make me a bodybuilder. There's a chance I could be—if I trained hard and developed the proper mindset. But I'm not one now.

In the same way that wish, identification, and routine don't automatically produce a bodybuilder, these same things don't necessarily make one a hot Christian. No matter how you wish to identify, you're either hot, cold, or lukewarm as a believer. Those who are hot in their walk with the Lord are constantly feeding on the Words of Christ and passionately sharing them with others to encourage them. Those believers who are cold have rejected the riches of grace that Christ offers. The lukewarm are those unfortunate believers who feel they have enough spiritual credit to coast through life, skimming the pages of Scripture to make sure they can still answer a few questions in Sunday school without looking clueless, but lacking any depth or passion in their walk.

Reheating Your Relationship

The Ephesian church in Revelation 2 had many things going well for them. They were commended for believing and doing the right things. They likely had the wish, identification, and routine of hot Christians. But God calls them lukewarm, and despite the good things they were doing, they were called upon to repent. They were described as "fallen," and were warned that their candlestick could be removed because of their being lukewarm. Their crime? Losing their first love.

When we sacrifice our lives to convenience and comfort rather than worshiping God and loving Him with our whole being, we've lost our first love.

We need to remember, through worship, the thrill of the gospel — that God the Son came from heaven and destroyed the power of sin and death by taking our punishment on the cross for our sins. In losing our first love, we violate the greatest commandment. This is serious and calls for repentance.

All of us have been there in our spiritual journey, and will probably be there again. We also have Christian friends who are complacent and need stimulation, or who are young and need exhortation to help them grow.

Our faith will flounder in the swamps of staleness until we regularly take note of who God says He is. We need not bother with who we want Him to be or who we naturally think He is apart from Scripture. In fact, if we yield our minds to these inaccuracies, we'll be at best a wandering Christian, and at worst, apostate. We must leave such things behind in our quest to remember our first love and press on toward knowing God fully — and His weight of glory. The Hebrew word in the Old Testament for glory is most often *kabod* (or *kavod*), which is closely related to the Hebrew word *kabad*, meaning heavy or weighty. This is no coincidence. God's glory is not to be taken lightly. Esteeming His glory for what it is will help us to revive that first love in our hearts.

The opposite of realizing God's gloriousness or heaviness is taking Him lightly. As God says, "I will honor those who honor me, but those who despise me will be cursed!" (1 Samuel 2:30). The word "despise" in today's usage usually denotes an active hatred. Here it's referring to a carelessness or taking something lightly. The context is the sins of Eli's two sons, Hophni and Phineas, who used their office as priests to their own advantage. Eli half-heartedly rebuked them for their sins, but failed to esteem the Lord more than his own household. According to the law, those sons should have been killed for their irreverence, but Eli failed to see the importance of honoring God above all. The result of their disrespect to the Lord was death for the sons and the destruction of Eli and his household.

Although one might be tempted to put a wide gulf of difference between our modern-day irreverence and that of Hophni and Phineas, make no mistake that the Lord is zealous of His glory (Isaiah 48:9-11). He's as zealous of His glory on weekdays as He is on Sunday. He's as zealous of His glory when we're trying to fit in with work colleagues as He is when we're with believers. Work, leisure, church, family, friends—He's always zealous of His glory. Our worship of Him is a bellwether of whether we take Him lightly or not. We can be sure our worship will be shallow or absent when we take God lightly. Focusing in worship on God's glorious attributes, His mighty works, and His relationship with us will reheat that first love and bring our souls to understand the weight of His greatness.

I encourage you to focus on an aspect of God's character you don't naturally comprehend. Most of us are quite comfortable with certain aspects of God's character and less comfortable with other aspects. Those aspects that we're comfortable with often become subjects for familiarity and irreverence.

For instance, many of us are comfortable with God's love. That's a good thing. God's love for each of us is unlike anything else in this world. It's unconditional, undeserved, unrestrained, and limitless. Since we're all familiar with a type of love generically, we have a frame of reference for understanding God's love at a certain level. However, if we study, meditate on, and worship only that which we understand (love, in this instance), we're at risk of becoming overly familiar and dangerously comfortable with it. Boredom and apathy set in, and our relationship grows cold.

So if God's love is what you're comfortable trying to grasp, focus on His holiness in prayer, worship, and meditation. This will expand the boundaries of your understanding about God, and will illuminate your heart to worship Him more fully, reigniting your first love. Likewise, if you're comfortable with God's justice in punishing sinners, focus on His mercy to us. What lover of food would restrict himself to hamburgers only, even if he loves hamburgers? Or what artist would paint a sunset using only one color?

Selah

Your kingdom is an eternal kingdom, and your dominion endures through all generations.

The Lord supports all who fall, and lifts up all who are bent over.

Everything looks to you in anticipation, and you provide them with food on a regular basis.

You open your hand, and fill every living thing with the food they desire.

The Lord is just in all his actions, and exhibits love in all he does.

The Lord is near all who cry out to him, all who cry out to him sincerely.

He satisfies the desire of his loyal followers; he hears their cry for help and delivers them.

The Lord protects those who love him, but he destroys all the wicked.

My mouth will praise the Lord.

Let all who live praise his holy name forever!
(Psalm 145:13-21)

Worship in Primary, Secondary, and Tertiary Colors

It's the experience of most men in this world to remark about the color of an object only to be corrected by a nearby woman. Most men see things in primary and (if lucky) secondary colors, but women see thousands of different colors—probably some that don't even exist. As the husband of a color enthusiast and the brother of an interior designer, I've learned to keep silent about colors. Who knew that there were so many shades of red? Merlot, apple, magenta, cherry, ruby, blood, etc. To me, they mostly just look like red. I feel that I should get at least a participation trophy for being able to distinguish that salmon and rose are pinks rather than reds. To most women, however, it's nearly criminal to call fuchsia "red" or crimson "red."

Satire aside, what a lavishing God we have! He not only created all those combinations of colors but allows us to see them with our eyes and interpret them with our brains. His world is meant to be seen in millions of different colors. He could have easily created the world in black and white, or even with shades of grey. Or He could have created objects with color yet left our eyes unable to see them.

In our eyes, we have photoreceptors in our retinas that are for low contrast (rods) and high contrast (cones). The cones send color signals to the brain. God gave us not just one type of cone, but three types—one for blues, one for greens and yellows, and one for reds. This allows us to see all the many colors around us and to enjoy the beauty of God's creation.

When we're young Christians, we often see God in primary colors. God is holy, God is loving, God is merciful, God is just. This may apply not only to young Christians but also to those who've never purposefully meditated on God's attributes while studying the Scriptures. Think back to the first few times you worshiped in prayer. Each time of praise was probably similar—worshiping God for the three or four attributes that easily stood out to you.

We may know more of God's attributes than three or four, but acknowledging them might not be easy for us, similar to knowing that magenta and burgundy are different, but calling them both "red" for ease. We should move past this. Imagine praising someone you love for the same three virtues every time. That person would probably get bored with your praise, wishing you would notice more nuance in their character and personality.

I don't think God ever tires of hearing our heartfelt worship, no matter how unskilled or lacking in variety it is. Red is beautiful. Holiness is awe-inspiring. Green is vibrant. Unconditional love is stirring. But when we search the Scriptures for the cerise and chartreuse of God's character, our construct of His indescribable nature takes on more detail of His reality.

Read Colossians 1:15-17 and worship God for His self-existence. Read Jeremiah 23:23-24 and worship God for His constant nearness to us. Read Nahum 1 and 2 Thessalonians 1:5-10 and worship God for His wrathfulness toward sin. Read Romans 8:15-17 and worship Him for His adoption of us into His family not as servants, but as children.

The Bible contains over 31,000 verses for good reason. If God wanted all our knowledge of Him to fit into a few pithy sayings and have all our prayers be thirty seconds long and homogeneous, He might have given the Bible to us in a thirty-slide PowerPoint presentation. Use every one of those 31,000-plus verses to learn the nuances of His character, praying for illumination by the Spirit and then praising Him as His spiritual treasures of wisdom overflow in our lives.

When we're exploring the Scriptures to find different facets of God's character, we must be careful to avoid two things. The first is the neglect of attributes that are unappealing to you, such as God's wrath and justice. If these are uncomfortable for you, study the Scriptures with good hermeneutics to reconcile questions about God's character that don't match with your mental construct of Him. At the end of the day, we must sometimes realize that even after a thorough study of Scripture, we may not be able to comprehend everything about our infinite and transcendent God, and we must yield to the ultimate authority of what Scripture says.

The second thing we must avoid is creating attributes of God that aren't delineated in Scripture. God is not a cosmic vending machine. He's not dependent on us for anything. We should be careful to not create things about Him that we *wish* to believe, but should worship what the Scriptures have revealed.

Use Worship in All Parts of Prayer

One of the many reasons that I think we struggle to worship is that we expect the worship part of our prayers to be a certain length. Maybe part of our problem is assuming that worship is a designated section of our prayer time, or that we need a worshipful soliloquy to use in conversation.

Many prayers in Scripture have worship intermingled throughout them. Filling our prayers with worship adds much more color to a dreary prayer life than if we merely confess for five minutes, ask for things for five minutes, intercede for five minutes, and give thanks for five minutes, all before bed — because we think we're supposed to pray this way. But it's better for our prayer life if we stay more mindful of who we're talking to when we confess sins or ask for things.

For instance, when we confess our sins to God, it would do well for us to remember not only His holiness and hatred of sin, but also His love, kindness, and mercy toward us. This is the only way to approach a transcendent and preeminent Sovereign of the universe.

Meditate for a day on Esther 4:9-17 and 5:1-4. In the time of King Ahasuerus, it was punishable by death for anyone to come before him unsummoned. Because of this, Esther prepared her approach to the king with much prayer and fasting, even commanding her people to pray and fast with her for three days. She then put on her royal robes, wishing to display her reverence for the king before even a word was uttered from her mouth. But notice that her preparation at that time was not for her to request the king's intervention on behalf of her people. It was simply for inviting the king to a banquet. Or more precisely, her preparation was really for her simply to approach the king and come into his presence spontaneously. The book of Esther is a beautiful story of wisdom, courage, and faith.

You and I will probably never stand uninvited before a king and risk losing our head over it. But we can still learn so much from this account. If Esther prayed and fasted along with all her people for three days in preparation to go before a king who owned none of the universe and had power to kill only her body, how much more should we approach the throne of the sovereign Lord of the universe with reverence, humility, and worship. Of course, this same Sovereign of the universe is our Abba Father, and the veil has been torn by our Intercessor, giving us unlimited access to the throne so we may come boldly before the throne of grace.

Daniel's prayer in Daniel 9 is a beautiful example, which I encourage you to read in its entirety. His prayer is one of personal and corporate confession. He starts out praying, "O Lord, great and awesome God who is faithful to His covenant with those who love Him and keep His commandments..." (9:4). As He proceeds to confess his personal sins and the sins of His people, he continually glorifies God for His righteousness, compassion, forgiveness, justice, power, fame, and abundant compassion (in 9:7-18). God owes His forgiveness to no one, so it's good to remember and praise His character in allowing us to come to Him and ask forgiveness of our sins.

Another great example is Psalm 51, one of the most beautiful chapters in the Bible. Here we see a man who has committed adultery and murder falling before the Lord and begging for His forgiveness. David begins,

> *Have mercy on me*, O God, because of your loyal love!
> Because of your great compassion, wipe away my rebellious
> acts! (51:1)

David worships God's loyal love and great compassion, realizing that these attributes are the reason he's able to come before a holy God and ask for forgiveness. He begs for mercy for his rebellious acts, not daring to minimize his transgressions or let himself off easy. This is the essence of confession and repentance—the stark realization and acknowledgment of God's absolute highness and our absolute depravity.

If we don't realize the impeccability of God's nature when we confess our sins, our confession becomes contrived, then emotionless, then absent. Additionally, it causes us to confess only what we feel guilty about, rather than any action on our part that's contrary to the nature of God.

Confession and repentance aren't merely negative feelings associated with the publicizing of our sins or our self-awareness of failure. Rather, they're the awareness of how we've missed the mark. Confession and repentance are not only for the big sins of gossip, envy, and hatred, but also for the times we ate too much, failed to listen to the Holy Spirit's prompts to witness, or promised in vain that we would pray for someone.

David goes on to worship God in verse 4 for His righteousness and justice, and in verse 7 for His sanctifying power. We see David confess his sin completely, then praise God in worship and gratitude:

> *Rescue me from the guilt of murder, O God, the God who delivers me! Then my tongue will shout for joy because of your deliverance. O LORD, give me the words! Then my mouth will praise you.* (51:14-15)

Look also at David's prayer of supplication in Psalm 86. He starts with pleas for God to save him, preserve him, and be gracious to him. Again, we don't see David focus on himself and his desires, but rather on God as he worshipfully prays:

Certainly O Lord, you are kind and forgiving, and show great faithfulness to all who cry out to you.... None can compare to you among the gods, O Lord! Your exploits are incomparable! All the nations, whom you created, will come and worship you, O Lord. They will honor your name. For you are great and do amazing things. You alone are God. (Psalm 86:5,8-10)

So we see that worship shouldn't be relegated only to a particular section of prayer. For our spirit to be right before the Lord when we come to Him in prayer, we must worship. For our confession, intercession, and supplication to be in the right spirit, we must worship.

Study Questions

1. Assess your worship life. Is it black and white? Primary colors? Tertiary colors?

2. How do you prepare to come before the Lord's throne?

3. Read Psalm 100. What ways are mentioned of how we're to come before the Lord's throne?

Chapter 14
Obstacles to Worship

When I was in college, I decided I was going to learn to salsa dance. After all, I loved both salsa music and swing dancing. If I could combine the two, I'd be one happy dancer.

This should work, I thought as I entered the gym where the Latin Dance Society was meeting. *I have good rhythm and can learn footwork. I'm decent at swing dancing and I'm pretty athletic. What can go wrong?*

Inside the gym, I realized that of the twenty-five or so college kids who were there, I was about half a foot taller than the next tallest person, and several shades paler.

A few kind people started showing me the basic steps. *Hey, this is pretty easy,* I thought as I picked my feet up and down learning the basic footwork. The president of the dance society, a fiery young woman standing at about four-feet-eleven, came over to me and said, "Hey, loosen up! We're all friends here!" I told her I was having fun, and that I felt pretty loose. She said I looked stiff as a board, to which I replied that this was about as loose as I could get. She then decided to take me on as her personal project to get me dancing more fluidly.

Although she was an incredibly accomplished dancer herself, and she did get me to dance a bit more artistically, she eventually gave up. There was nothing about me that suggested I'd ever dance without looking like I was wearing a dirty diaper.

I kept trying. It took me a full four weeks just to barely locate the muscles that could move my hips. The desire was certainly there.

Some of the basics were even there. There were just too many obstacles keeping me from ever looking halfway decent.

In our journey to worship God as we should, sometimes it's not enough to have a desire to worship and a basic understanding of what we're supposed to be doing. Sometimes we must remove obstacles that hinder us. There are many obstacles to worship—some insidious, and some vicious and powerful.

Self-Worship

This is a rare weapon that seems to be just as effective against the child of God as it is against the children of the world. Like many weapons of the devil, there was an ancient prototype that's upgraded in potency and subtilty with every new generation of humanity. It's so well camouflaged that most are unaware of its existence around them or in them, and those who are aware are able to easily rationalize it. The model that plagues today's generation is particularly subtle, to the point that the devilish whispers promoting their product are now coming from people both within Christianity and without.

Make no mistake, subtlety doesn't imply benignity. Throughout history, this ancient weapon has caused an unbelievable amount of carnage, both physical and spiritual. It's what drove Adam and Eve to eat the fruit in the garden. It's what drove Cain to kill his brother Abel. It caused Esau to relinquish his birthright, and Saul to disobey God and have the kingdom ripped from him. It caused David to commit adultery and murder, Judas to betray Christ, and Peter to deny Him.

It has caused the wealthy to obsessively pursue more riches, and the powerful to ruthlessly pursue more power. In the thirteenth century, it drove England's King John to murder his nephew, cheat his barons, and renege on his promises in the Magna Carta. Centuries later it caused slaveholders in America to treat their slaves like animals, and King Leopold II of Belgium to maim and kill the

Congolese for his personal gain, and Hitler to kill his way to his Aryan dreams.

Today, it causes us to gossip about others, to complain about our circumstances, and to care more about our social media showcase than our ambassadorship of Christ. It is euphemized by Christians as "not wanting to offend" others with the gospel, and rationalized by saying that God wants us to enjoy our time on earth.

This world—including even our Christian culture—is rife with self-worship. It does everything to derail our relationship with God and to keep us from fulfilling our sacred purpose of being God-worshipers. Worship of God is a sweet-smelling offering to Him, but self-worship is like sticking our faces in a rotting carcass.

Though it comes in many shapes and sizes in today's culture, the current model seems to be worship of self-esteem. It keeps us quiet about the Lord because we don't want to feel embarrassed or puerile. It prioritizes our feeling good about ourselves above God's mission for us. It exalts our glory above God's glory.

There's no such thing as low self-esteem. Low self-esteem is really self-exaltation. If esteem of ourselves were truly low, we would take joy when life plagues us with misadventures. If we don't esteem someone else, we sinfully take joy at their demise. When an unethical boss who has done us wrong gets divorced, we inwardly cheer the cosmic justice. Meanwhile, we don't readily bask in our own trials and hardships as we would those of someone else we truly despise. I doubt that anyone ever thought, "I'm so glad I got all my money taken from me; it serves me right," or "I'm so glad the person I wanted to marry broke up with me; maybe next time I won't be so stupid."

The Bible comments, "For no one has ever hated his own body but he feeds it and takes care of it" (Ephesians 5:29). Self-hate is really an ardent wish that we would be exalted and a despair that we are not.

Of course, mental illness is real, and I'm not discrediting

depression or dysthymia. Sometimes "feeling bad" is a physical disease that must be treated physically. Sometimes it's a spiritual disease that must be treated spiritually. But the treatment of "low self-esteem" should never been centered upon raising our opinions of ourselves. We already think we deserve much better than we do, and we wish to be exalted by others as we exalt ourselves.

We're prime suspects for Satan's third temptation of Christ—to be exalted by the world and have the power the world gives. The empty promises of this temptation are that we deserve adulation, and that receiving it will bring fulfillment in life and higher self-esteem. What it really does is unseat Christ's lordship in our lives. We spend our time seeking self-fulfillment in worldly things when only a closer walk with the Lord can fulfill us. We spend time and energy thinking about how to make more money, or to garner more attention through how we dress or look, or to obtain more affirmation from social media. None of these things fulfill us.

We always desire more of what we worship. When we worship money, sex, power, prestige, or affirmation, we find ourselves wanting more of the lies and death they have to offer. When we worship the living God, we find ourselves wanting more of the bright glory and abundant life He has to offer.

The worshiper who fills all her spiritual vision with the bright colors of God's glory leaves no room for self-worship. She denies herself and takes up her cross, worshiping along the way. Although we're sometimes tempted to worship ourselves through our accomplishments, Paul said this about his own achievements:

> *But these assets I have come to regard as liabilities because of Christ. More than that, I now regard all things as liabilities compared to the far greater value of knowing Christ Jesus my Lord, for whom I have suffered the loss of all things—indeed, I regard them as dung!—that I may gain Christ.* (Philippians 3:7-8)

Paul knew that God on the throne is of utmost importance. Only God's greatness and glory can satisfy us. Everything else in this world—self-worship included—only leaves us wanting more. This is why God is so loving when He desires that we worship Him. John Piper famously said, "God is most glorified in us when we are most satisfied in Him." But we can experience the total fulfillment He brings only when we worship Him alone—not self, and not things. Total satisfaction means that all our worship is directed toward Him.

John the Baptist says it like this, regarding Jesus: "He must increase and I must decrease" (John 3:30). Here was a prophet of God, spoken of in the Old Testament, and of whom Jesus said that no one greater had ever been born of a woman. John the Baptist might easily have said of Jesus, "He must increase a lot, while I increase only a little." Or, "I must be great so I can make Him greater." But John knew that the Lord deserves *all* the glory. Not a share of it, or most of it—but *all*.

He must increase, and we must decrease.

Busyness

The church is too busy with things of the world. Generally, I've found that God's people can be divided into three categories: those who think busier is better, those caught up in the rat race and unintentionally too busy, and those who only think they're too busy.

Ask a brother or sister at church how they've been, and a typical reply is "Busy." It's sad that we've glorified and rationalized busyness. Originally, God intended us for walks in the garden with Him. If we're overly busy, shouldn't we be ashamed to tell someone at church, "I've been too busy this week"?

We easily forget these wise words from Solomon:

If the Lord does not build a house, then those who build it work in vain. If the Lord does not guard a city, then the watchman stands guard in vain. It is vain for you to rise

early, come home late, and work so hard for your food. Yes,
he can provide for those whom he loves even when they sleep.
(Psalm 127:1-2)

Even being busy with good things—working to take care of and
provide for our families, serving the Lord, and being good stewards
of our possessions—can all be detrimental to our walk with the Lord.
(Imagine if Adam had told God, "I'm too busy keeping the garden to
meet with you," or, "These animals won't name themselves.")

In Luke 10:38-42, we see how Martha was too busy serving the
Lord to enjoy His presence. Honestly, in today's church, we would
probably give her our Member of the Year award. We're told that
Martha welcomed the Lord into her house, then did her best in all-
consuming preparations for serving Him well. Frazzled by this, she
came to the Lord and asked Him to tell Mary to help her. One could
truthfully say that she was hospitable and service-minded, and that
she encouraged others toward service. There's no evidence that her
heart intended evil toward her sister. We don't detect that she was
trying to impress anyone out of pride. Everything seemed right.

In responding to Martha's request to her sister, the Lord doesn't
condemn Martha's heart. Instead, he gently exposes her unwise
choice of doing things for Him instead of basking in His glorious
presence. The Lord gives the honor to Mary, who sat at His feet and
listened to His message. Remember the concept of *proskyneo*?
Although this isn't the word used here, the idea is similar. Mary is
revering the Lord, taking time to hear His message, hanging onto
every word He says, enraptured in His presence. Essentially, worship
is the difference between Mary and Martha. Presumably, they both
loved Jesus, but that day, only Mary sat at His feet in humble
adulation.

Again, the most important thing a believer can know is that this
life isn't the ultimate reality. Knowing this will influence the way we
spend our time and worship the Lord. If this life is the ultimate
reality, we should spend our time improving the world at the expense

of knowing God. If this life is more real than the next, we should marginalize time with the Lord ("We'll have plenty of time to worship Him in eternity") in favor of gaining earthly advantage. But if we're convinced that heaven is our true reality, we'll be obsessed with preparing for it—learning how to worship the Lord, and building up our lives with spiritual gold, silver, and precious jewels as we learn the heart of the Lord. Even the "secular" activities we undertake will become sacred. Our jobs will become channels for sharing the glory of the Lord's gospel with others. Our leisure time will be spent with praise and thanksgiving to the Lord. We'll stand in awe of Him at the sight of a sunset or rainbow. We'll realize the truths of Psalm 127:1-2—that apart from God, our pursuits are in vain and our busyness is wasted.

Fortunately or unfortunately, we cannot lie to ourselves about whether we're living for this life or the next. Our day-planners, our conversations, and our internet browser history tell us the truth with brutal succinctness.

I cannot tell you how to become less busy in a way that will glorify God. It's possible to cut out every mandatory event in your day and still be too busy to spend time with Him. However, I am certain that in knowing and worshiping Him, you'll want more of Him, and the more of Him you want, the less of the world's busyness you'll want. You'll long to be in God's presence, basking in His glorious attributes with all the time that eternity has to offer.

God is in no hurry to show Himself to us. Let's embrace homesickness and even hope to catch more of it. Being homesick for heaven makes it painful to pry ourselves away from our prayerful worshiping of Him.

Selah

"I am the Alpha and the Omega," says the Lord God— the one who is, and who was, and who is still to come—the All-Powerful! (Revelation 1:8)

From east to west the LORD's name is deserving of praise.

The LORD is exalted over all the nations; his splendor reaches beyond the sky.

Who can compare to the LORD our God, who sits on a high throne?

He bends down to look at the sky and the earth.

He raises the poor from the dirt, and lifts up the needy from the garbage pile, that he might seat him with princes, with the princes of his people.

He makes the barren woman of the family a happy mother of children.

Praise the LORD! (Psalm 113:3-9)

Distraction

Of all the insulting things that can happen to a physician, a patient taking a non-urgent call during the visit is one of the worst. I don't mind if people ask for second opinions, or even if they contradict me because of what they've read on the internet. Both of those show that at least the patient is engaged. But when people take a non-urgent phone call during my visit with them—especially if they're chatting for several minutes—that causes a problem for me. I used to sit politely or work on the encounter note while they finished their conversation about the new series on TV, or about a purple dress the person wants to buy. Now I just leave the room and see a different patient. It's not that I feel I'm too good to be treated in such a way, or that my time is more valuable than theirs. But what I have to tell them about their health is important, and I don't want it to get subjugated by the purple dress. I want my conversation with them to hold their attention so they remember it. Therefore, sometimes I have to come back when they're not distracted and completely reset the conversation. Otherwise, they could end up losing their vision.

How often do we do the same thing with God? We enter His throne room — the throne room of the great King of the universe, our loving Father, who forsook His Son as the sacrifice for our sins so that He could have an intimate relationship with us. Then we let ourselves be called away from our face-to-face meeting with Him by a text message, or our remembering a good or bad conversation the night before. Or by music. Or hunger. Or that email we forgot to write yesterday. Or the work problem gnawing at our minds. Or news and sports websites. Or sometimes even by journaling about our time with God, or by even preparing a Bible study from it. Suddenly our time with the Lord is over, and our overly busy day starts. And we wonder why our time with the Lord is dry and we're not hearing from Him. Why our worship life isn't flourishing.

The Scriptures will speak to us if we take undistracted time to listen. But we've learned to accept distracted brief glances of our Savior when we need attentive gazes at Him that will transform us into His likeness and teach us to sing His praises. Why do we accept these distractions over the life-giving worship of God?

Since the beginning of time, the devil and his minions have wreaked havoc on humanity by offering us things that seem innocent, so much so that we often don't realize we're being tempted. Think of the fruit in the garden; what's so wrong with taking a bite? How about turning stones into loaves of bread? Jesus certainly did much more impressive things than that during His ministry, so why not turn stones into bread? How about a tirade of despair against God when all your possessions, family, and health have been taken from you, as happened to Job?

When we think our time in God's throne room has escaped the evil one's notice, and that the distractions are only coincidental, we've already lost the battle. When we're in the middle of our worship, it's unlikely that a liquor bottle will suddenly appear in front of us — though getting drunk would suddenly bring an end to our time of worship. Rather, a small distraction is all it takes to derail us, and it's something we don't recognize as ruining our spiritual life. After all, most of the distractions are reasonable interruptions if they occurred in a different context. Once again, a favorite tactic of the tempter. If Eve had eaten any other fruit in the garden, it would have been fine. If Christ had been in His public ministry and Satan were not whispering in His ear that He should provide for Himself apart from the Father's will, it would have been fine for Christ to turn stones into bread. So it's not that the items distracting us are evil in themselves. Rather, familiar things are used by the evil one trying to lead us away from God.

Agenda

An interesting social phenomenon is when a person with little knowledge and experience in a subject will dominate a conversation with someone who's an expert in the field. For an onlooker, it's amusing to see the foolish one "instruct" the learned; it usually leads to a good story and a few laughs. For the learned individual (depending on how wise he or she is), the range of response varies greatly from gracious patience to extreme frustration. Meanwhile the unwisely talkative individual notices nothing.

One of the most dangerous things we can do in our spiritual life—something that will stunt our growth and inhibit worship—is to approach our relationship with the Lord with an agenda. To talk instead of listening. To instruct the Lord when we should be silent. Ecclesiastes 5:1 states it well: "Be careful what you do when you go to the temple of God; draw near to listen rather than to offer a sacrifice like fools, for they do not realize that they are doing wrong."

We all do this. If we routinely limit our time in the Word to fit into our busy schedules, and we know which two chapters we'll read, and we have our multiple-step process to become closer to God, and we have a witnessing "target" in mind, and we've served our church in the same limited way for the past ten years—we may be approaching our walk with an agenda. This is not to disparage organization. In one aspect, worship is a discipline that requires discipline, especially for the undisciplined. But when we don't get past the point of discipline (or ritual, in some cases), we grasp the microphone and throw away the earphones. The words we skillfully contrive ring hollow. We notice nothing, just as the fools in Ecclesiastes 5:1 fail to realize they're doing evil. There's no illumination of the Spirit, no breath of life, no adventure led by the Spirit. Things of God are either dry or seem fake to us. The world seems more real to us than the Word.

The Lord gifts us all with different personalities; some of us thrive with a written to-do list, and others find it restrictive or petty. It's not that list-keepers can't truly worship. But their temptation is to attempt worship without the whispers of the Holy Spirit, which is vital for true worship.

Ephesians 5:18-20 centers on our being filled with the Holy Spirit. The worship, encouragement, and thanksgiving that are taught in this passage all result from being filled with the Spirit. We often think of listening to the Holy Spirit when making large decisions or doing things that scare us, such as witnessing or refraining from bungee jumping. But our approach to the Word, prayer, and worship should also be in attentiveness to the Spirit. This is not some trance-like emptying of our minds, but rather mulling Scripture mentally, and praying scriptural truth to the Lord. It means asking the Lord to show us things from Scripture about Himself. Reflecting on His goodness and greatness before we pray. Listening to the stirrings and convictions of the Spirit. Recounting His interventions in our lives. The more we listen for the Spirit in every aspect of our lives, the more we'll hear Him. We'll learn to say, "Not my will, but Yours be done."

Feeling Shame

The feeling of shame is real. I would love to pretend that it isn't, and that if you're mature in the faith you won't experience embarrassment when you speak of the Lord in public. While the feeling of shame may decrease with maturity, there'll always be some amount of self-awareness when we worship in front of other people outside the expected realm of normality. We may feel shame with even a short mention of God to unbelievers, not wanting to be categorized as a Jesus freak. Or, unfortunately, we may feel shame from believers if we gush about God in conversation with them, or in front of them in prayer. Who hasn't criticized the person who prays for a longer duration than we think fit? Or the one whose prayer is more flowery than we think is reasonable?

The feeling of shame is a major barrier to worshiping in conversation or public prayer. It's also a major barrier for our witness to others. However, this is a chance to experience His overwhelming grace as we turn our backs on the idle comforts of this world and identify with Christ. This is the grace the writer of Hebrews speaks of:

> *Therefore let us confidently approach the throne of grace to receive mercy and find grace whenever we need help.* (Hebrews 4:16)

Christian couch potatoes don't receive generous helpings of God's in-time-of-need grace. It's by His grace poured into our lives that we grow in the faith. If we can overcome feelings of shame in expressing to God and others our relationship with Christ, by God's grace we'll grow. The church will grow.

Take note, however, that if you struggle with embarrassment, winning this battle won't happen overnight. It takes many attempts and many failures to get to the point where your brain and mouth don't hinder your spirit. Keep pressing on. Worship that's completely internal or that consists of only fifteen minutes each Sunday morning (when it actually brings shame to *not* worship) calls into question the true depth of our knowledge of Him.

Here are some thoughts that will help us overcome the feeling of shame.

Only a Feeling

First, that feeling of shame is only that. It's not actually *being* ashamed, and it's not a good reason to hold silent.

Don't confuse feeling ashamed with being ashamed. Throughout the Scriptures, we see men who had opportunity to give God glory, but then failed. Jesus addresses our feeling nervous about defending our faith in Luke 12:11, where He says, "Do not worry about how you should make your defense or what you should say." He knows our hearts and our tendencies, yet rather than condemn our lack of boldness, He offers assurance of being taught by the Holy Spirit.

The sin is not in our being scared; the sin is yielding to the shame and staying quiet. It's like many other tendencies—heterosexual attraction, homosexual attraction, drinking, over-working, etc. The sin is not in the tendency, but in giving in to those tendencies through our lust, adultery, practicing homosexuality, drunkenness, workaholism, etc.

We shouldn't feel guilty about the increased blood pressure and funny feeling in our stomach combined with our brains telling us not to publicly give glory to God or witness. But when those normal tendencies are allowed to keep us quiet, that's where the sin occurs. It occurs when we value our glory above God's. Our temporal comfort above lost souls' destinations. Our self-esteem above God's esteem.

While you may not think that the feeling of shame is keeping you quiet, most of our excuses to keep silent are mere cover-ups for the feeling of shame. Here are some of those excuses we use (although they aren't usually the real issue):

> The time isn't right.
> The person would likely not be interested.
> I don't know what to say, and it might make the Lord
> look silly.
> I didn't feel the Holy Spirit leading me.

All these are excuses I've perfected. But they aren't good ones. There's no valid excuse against the prompting of the Holy Spirit.

Some are so adept at making excuses that they're convinced the Holy Spirit rarely prompts them. But He *is* prompting. He's the same Holy Spirit who prompted Peter to take on all the religious leaders, knowing that he could lose his life. The same Holy Spirit who prompted Paul to speak in every synagogue he came to. The same Holy Spirit who led Philip to walk up to the Ethiopian eunuch and ask if he understood what he was reading.

The Holy Spirit is prompting you. Every single day He prompts. But will we listen?

The excuses make us dull to His prompting. We blanket a year's worth of encounters with a single excuse: "That cashier is just trying to do his job, and I don't want to force God on Him." With that single excuse, we shut down all the promptings of the Holy Spirit every time we go to the store, until there's intervention upon that excuse. We waste millions of words and years of our lives living in the mediocrity of noble excuses.

Instead, publicly worship the Lord—and witness for Him.

Christ Bore Our Shame

A second factor for overcoming our sense of shame is that Christ experienced shame for us. None of us will ever know what it's like to lay aside infinite glory in order to do what Christ did. It's far beyond the illustration of a potter becoming clay. Furthermore, what could be more humiliating than coming as a naked, crying baby? Throughout His life and ministry, He was disciplined erroneously by His parents, misunderstood, and even forsaken by friends and family. The religious leaders hated Him. He knew their thoughts of hatred and conspiracy against Him, yet engaged them for the purpose of the gospel.

Jesus experienced the fickleness of humanity—the people He'd healed and taught, the people He'd come to serve. He was mocked and spat upon, and given an unjust trial. Then came the cross, where he died a prolonged and excruciating death as a criminal in front of jeering crowd.

Worship and witness should never be motivated by guilt. But from love, rather than guilt, we can say, "Christ experienced shame for us; therefore we can experience shame for him."

We can draw from His thirty-three years of humility, being certain that Jesus knows what it's like to feel shame. Therefore He tells us that "we can say with confidence, 'The Lord is my helper, and I will not be afraid. What can people do to me?'" (Hebrews 13:6).

For we do not have a high priest incapable of sympathizing with our weaknesses, but one who has been tempted in every way just as we are, yet without sin. (Hebrews 4:15).

Selah

Do you not know? Have you not heard?

The LORD is an eternal God, the Creator of the whole earth.

He does not get tired or weary; there is no limit to his wisdom.

He gives strength to those who are tired; to the ones who lack power, he gives renewed energy. Isa 40:28-29

O Lord, you have been our protector through all generations!

Even before the mountains came into existence, or you brought the world into being, you were the eternal God. (Psalm 90:1-2)

This Is for You

A third reason for overcoming any feeling of shame is the certainty that glorifying the Lord to Him and to others is for *you*. Regardless of your spiritual gift, worship and witness are for *you*. However embarrassed you feel when talking to people about God, worship and witness are for *you*. Whether you're introverted or extroverted, worship and witness are for *you*. Whether you're eloquent or inarticulate, worship and witness are for *you*. Even if you're new to the faith, worship and witness are for *you*.

When Jesus healed the Gadarene demoniac, He commanded this spiritual novice to return to his own house and tell everyone there what God had done for him. The man did this and more. "He went away, proclaiming throughout the whole town what Jesus had done for him" (Luke 8:38-39).

No verses in Scripture relegate worship to certain demographics or personality types, or to possession of a certain spiritual gift. Once we unconditionally step out in faith from behind our curtain of hiding, the light and life of God's enabling will endow us with the strength to be bold ambassadors for Him. I want to highlight that this is stepping out *unconditionally*—because we cannot base our obedience to the Lord on how we felt about one experience, or on our perceived lack of fruit in the past. God is more pleased by a halting tongue used in submissive obedience than by a persuasive or eloquent tongue used in human strength.

As a child who jumps off the refrigerator into his father's arms may fear that he's jumping to his death, so we who aren't naturally gifted in evangelism have a special opportunity to throw ourselves off the cliff of reputation, entrusting ourselves to the loving arms of our Father, who will indeed catch us. It's a chance for intimacy with the Godhead: with the Father because of His promises to provide for us, with the Son because He knows our weakness, and with the Holy Spirit because He helps us know what to say in our hour of need.

When I struggle with witnessing, I'm helped by these words:

Therefore, since we are surrounded by such a great cloud of witnesses, we must get rid of every weight and the sin that clings so closely, and run with endurance the race set out for us, keeping our eyes fixed on Jesus, the pioneer and perfecter of our faith. For the joy set out for him he endured the cross, disregarding its shame, and has taken his seat at the right hand of the throne of God. Think of him who endured such opposition against himself by sinners, so that you may not grow weary in your souls and give up. (Hebrews 12:1-3)

Inadequacy

One way that we might experience feeling shame when we vocalize worship and witness is in sensing our inadequacy. Whereas some may feel shame from others' disdain, others may feel shame in that we're inadequate to enter into God's Holy of Holies, given our wretchedly sinful condition. We may feel that God could never accept our sacrifice of worship because we've sinned and confessed in the same area every day for the last three years straight. We may feel that we would only mock the name of Christ in hypocrisy if we were to witness to a colleague who has seen us fail so many times. We think, "God can use me, but only after I clean up my act."

While this attitude may seem pious, it's anything but if we allow it to close our mouths. The truth is that none of us are worthy in and of ourselves either to enter into His presence in worship or to be His ambassadors. If we think we're worthy, then we don't understand the gospel. We're made worthy by the blood of Christ cleansing our sins and clothing us in His righteousness, apart from any inherent goodness of our own. And if we doubt that truth—then again, we don't understand the gospel.

To wallow in our inadequacy and allow it to shut us up can be traced to one of two sinful mindsets: self-pity and faithlessness.

Occasionally, I have patients who are convinced they're going blind, although many tests indicate otherwise. Despite my credentials and the worthiness of the tests, the patients aren't convinced that nothing's wrong with their eyes. In many of these cases, the patient is looking not for professional evaluation but for a listening ear to hear of their many "ailments." No amount of reassurance can convince them otherwise. They're bound and determined to assume the role of a sick person.

So it is with the believer unwilling to let go of the sin God has already removed from us. Such a person assumes the role of a spiritually sick person. They fail to realize that as far as the east is from the west, so God removes the guilt of our rebellious actions from us (Psalm 103:12).

Self-pity blinds us, even in the presence of our great and glorious God, to the awe and wonder of who He is. It turns our focus instead to our miserable sins, which God has assured us repeatedly are covered by the blood of His Son. Such a wrong perspective is true misery. The insidious nature of self-pity is that it will relentlessly try to convince you that you aren't worshiping yourself but are rather a victim of circumstances, mindset, or even a more "innocent" sin. If you suspect this in yourself, don't allow for excuses.

Self-pity masquerading as "inadequacy" is a common scourge among today's Christians. How can we tell this? It's because self-empowerment "praise songs" are much more popular than doctrinally rich praise songs that elucidate and reassure our position in Christ. If you struggle with self-pity disguised as feelings of inadequacy, it's so important that you don't feed the flesh by listening to songs and quotes of empowerment. That's exactly what your flesh desires. These songs often use truth from God's Word, but they place all the focus on you—insisting that you're beautiful, you're a work in progress, you're strong, you're loved, you're special. While such statements are based more or less on scriptural truth, they appeal to egocentrism when they're isolated simply to make us feel good about ourselves. They fuel the very obstacle to worship.

Faithlessness may seem more innocent, but is equally sinful and damaging. Those of us who struggle with this sin understand the conflict verbalized by the father of the demon-possessed boy who said, "I believe; help my unbelief" (Mark 9:24).

Although the evil one and sin will continually tell us we're unworthy to worship God and to witness of Him to others, we must fight this lie with the knowledge of the truth of God's character and promises. Once again, the antidote is found not in songs validating our worth, but in Scripture that relates the worthiness of Christ and His work on the cross for us, imputed to us by a holy and just God.

If anyone had reason to feel shame over his unworthiness, it would be David after his sin with Bathsheba and his murder of Uriah. In Psalm 51, he is utterly repentant over his sin, but not despondent in faithlessness. His repentance doesn't drive him away from God, but rather toward Him. His response of confession is filled with God's promises and with worship of God's character, rather than just trying to feel better about himself:

Have mercy on me, O God, because of your loyal love! Because of your great compassion, wipe away my rebellious acts! (51:1)

Sprinkle me with water and I will be pure; wash me and I will be whiter than snow. (51:7)

Rescue me from the guilt of murder, O God, the God who delivers me! Then my tongue will shout for joy because of your deliverance. O Lord, give me the words! Then my mouth will praise you. (51:14-15)

David was, of course, completely forgiven and restored. We're never partially forgiven for our sins. There are no dog ears associated with God's forgiveness, as if He would bookmark our sin to remind us of it after our ninety-sixth failure. His forgiveness is utter and complete because of Christ's righteousness imputed to us.

If believing in God's forgiveness is a struggle for you, meditate on God's mercy and forgiveness, and worship Him for these. Read of His justice and holiness that allow Christ's sacrifice to be accounted for us. Recount His many promises. We worship and witness in obedience, not in perceived self-worth.

A Low View of God

Not many of us would admit to having a low view of God. Maybe our conscious view of Him is high at times (especially during church), but our subconscious view of Him is mostly low, especially during the week. We're assured that "Jesus loves me, this I know," but we act like this truth is relevant only when we encounter serious struggles that our best efforts cannot control ("It's time to call in backup"). When this is the case, we're unlikely to be found worshiping the Lord on any given day that doesn't start with "S" and end with "unday."

Having a low view of God may not express itself as taking God's name in vain or speaking flippantly about Him. It may be more silently expressed in our mindset and priorities. In our minds, a low view of God exalts all the prior obstacles above the glory of the true God. We live as functional idol-worshipers, seeking joy and satisfaction in things we as believers know will not satisfy us. As long as there's no interruption in life, we see no reason to be on our knees constantly. When we feel big, we wrongfully see God as small.

Agur, who wrote Proverbs 30, was a wise man. He knew that God was too lofty for his understanding. Agur also knew that prosperity could result in spiritual complacency and a low view of God. He wrote this:

> *I have not learned wisdom, nor do I have knowledge of the Holy One. Who has ascended into heaven, and then descended? Who has gathered up the winds in his fists? Who has bound up the waters in his cloak? Who has established*

all the ends of the earth? What is his name, and what is his son's name? —if you know! (30:3-4)

And this:

Do not give me poverty or riches, feed me with my allotted portion of bread, lest I become satisfied and act deceptively and say, "Who is the LORD?" (30:8-9)

Prosperity may be a tangible progenitor of a low view of God, since all the riches of the world whisper in our ears that we need nothing more than them. But what's the spiritual condition that inspires us to this low view of God? It's likely either a poor and careless command of biblical doctrine or a lack of surrender to that doctrine.

When we don't know the God of the Bible as He reveals Himself through our careful study of theology and doctrine, we make Him out to be who we want Him to be. He ends up being much like ourselves in our minds. Because He's infinitely higher than we are, we're in danger of blasphemy and idolatry when we (sometimes unwittingly) make Him to be like us. We should therefore approach doctrine with the highest degree of interest and intensity. If we toss it aside to avoid conflict or ageless debates, we'll have a low view of God. We'll have bought nonconfrontation and laziness of mind at the high price of not knowing God as He has revealed Himself.

We're tempted to exchange the glory of the immortal God for an image resembling mortal human beings and worldly trinkets. After we've construed a completely false god and experienced its impotence, we *should* have a low view of it. In Isaiah 44, the prophet describes the stupidity of idol worship and how an idol-maker uses the same piece of wood to keep warm, cook over, and make his god. But a god who isn't perfect in virtue and excellence of character is not worthy of worship. A god who resembles myself is no more worthy of worship than is success, money, power, fleshly gratification, or comfort. An intense and honest study of the doctrines of the Bible will give us a higher view of God that leads us into worship.

Maybe you know well the doctrines of the Bible but you still feel that you have a low view of God obstructing your worship. Lack of surrender to the revelation of God's character is a common vice in the spiritually educated crowd. When we think "lack of surrender," we shouldn't think of the derelict who would rather wallow in a morally bankrupt lifestyle than acknowledge the existence of God. Think rather of the Sunday school teacher who spends hours per week searching the Scriptures for what his pupils need to hear, but neglects the very things Christ wants to grow in his own life. Or think of the Christian social media activist who spends more time arguing about how great God is than worshiping His greatness. Or the criticizer who can sniff out the spiritual problems in others and use them for teaching points, but doesn't see her own shortcomings. In those examples, the "spiritual" individual lives as though following Christ is similar to being in a country club. We say and do the right things, give some money, act like the Christians around us, and are satisfied. Those who know the "secret handshake" of Christianity are in—but those who don't should be witnessed to, or just prayed for, or at least told that they'll be prayed for. Lack of surrender can obviously take a variety of appearances.

Callousness to the gentle whisperings of the Holy Spirit, from whom worship flows, is a hallmark of nonsurrender. It doesn't have to be a willful rebellion, and it can be found even in truly godly individuals around us. It's not that there's no desire or love for the Lord, as there certainly can be. There's just decreased spiritual sensation as our head knowledge stays in our head and doesn't find its way to our hearts.

An unsurrendered believer is a spiritual zombie—not dead and yet lifeless, unloving, and unfeeling, lumbering about aimlessly, feeding off others' brains and spiritual intellects, and turning those around them into spiritual zombies.

Unfortunately, I'm not wise enough to instruct you how to deal with nonsurrender in a certain number of steps. Our calloused hearts need spiritual exfoliation in order to feel the stirrings of the Spirit, which cause us to fall at the foot of God's throne in worship. God brings brokenness into our lives so that we yearn for a taste of His glory and want nothing else but to bask in His presence. A few words of worship uttered at the foot of His throne from a broken spirit are far more valuable than all the things done on spiritual autopilot. If you dare, pray for brokenness in your life so that you can be truly captivated by God's absolute greatness and glory.

Apart from these obstacles, worship should come naturally for us as redeemed children of God indwelt by the Holy Spirit and saved for worship. Although there may be other obstacles to worship, being aware of those mentioned in this chapter should help us begin to know where we personally struggle and fail. Identify which of these is the most obvious obstacle for you, and pray that the Lord would help you overcome it. Take measures to remove it from your life, whether by writing notecards as a reminder, filling your mind with Scripture that teaches you how to defeat it, or taking willful steps to combat it.

All these obstacles to worship are also obstacles to other parts of our sanctification, so removing them from our lives will bring us closer to Christ's likeness and improve our spiritual health in other ways. We were redeemed at a price—and we should therefore tear down everything that hinders our glorification of God. Don't settle for anything less.

Study Questions

1. What are some potentially good things in your life that can be obstacles to your worship?

2. How can we tell if we're surrendered to God?

3. Read Acts 8:9-24. What are some obstacles to worship we can find in this passage?

Chapter 15

Building a Lifestyle of Worship

When the Son of God came to earth, He didn't come to enjoy His life here. Nor was this just a phase of His life when He was determined to "carpe diem." He came for a purpose.

He wasn't bringing an end to hunger and poverty. He wasn't trying to make humans play nice. He wasn't building any bank accounts or even trying to leave a legacy for Himself. Jesus reveals the true purpose of His life's work in John 17, where glory is mentioned eight times. Jesus's work during His ministry was to glorify the Father by making His name known on the earth (17:4,6). In turn, God the Father would glorify the Son by giving Him the glory He had before the world was created, and by allowing believers to share in His glorification (17:22,24).

In this prayer in John 17, we see Christ glorifying the Father, the Father glorifying Christ, Christ sharing His glory with believers, and believers glorifying Christ. If glorifying the Father is Christ's mission, and if His desire is that we see His glory that the Father has given to Him, then *our* mission is to glorify Christ and the Father. This is how worship, the gospel, and witnessing all fit together.

As we've seen, the gospel is rooted in worship. We cannot be saved from our sins if we don't acknowledge our utter depravity in contrast to God's holiness and transcendence. It's the concept of worshiping from the ground under God's footstool. If we elevate ourselves to the throne in self-worship or humanism, failing to realize the gravity of our sins, we cannot be saved. If we believe God to be less than He is, bringing Him down to our level as some sort of jolly pal or curve-grading teacher, we cannot be saved. When the gospel takes root, The first fruit of our salvation is worship.

All other parts of our spiritual journey on earth are about God's glory. When we worship, we're exalting God's glory to God. When we witness, we're exalting God's glory to unbelievers. When we fellowship, we're exalting God's glory to believers. Our obedience must be for God's glory, or else it's legalism. Our prayer must be according to God's glory, or else it becomes selfish and monotonous. Our time in the Word must be for the exaltation of God's glory, or else it's mere self-improvement.

Worship is foundational to the biblical fundamentals. It builds God's kingdom for His glory.

The Pleasure of Constancy

What a privilege to be called to dwell in the house of the majestic King of all things and to worship Him continually! When we walk into a great mansion and stand agape at its beauty, we might think to ourselves, "If I lived in this place, I would never leave it." That's the kind of feeling the sons of Korah communicate about being in the Lord's presence, in Psalm 84:

> *How lovely is the place where you live, O LORD who rules over all! I desperately want to be in the courts of the LORD's temple. My heart and my entire being shout for joy to the living God. Even the birds find a home there, and the swallow builds a nest, where she can protect her young near your altars, O LORD who rules over all, my king and my God. How blessed are those who live in your temple and praise you continually! Selah (Psalm 84:1-4)*

Being in the Lord's presence is no duty or chore. It should not be approached as a checklist of spiritual disciplines that we exercise. It's the pleasure that Anna, the prophetess experienced as she continuously dwelt in the tabernacle in prayer and fasting the vast majority of her life (Luke 2:37). It's a pleasure expressed centuries earlier by David:

I have asked the Lord for one thing—this is what I desire! I want to live in the Lord's house all the days of my life, so I can gaze at the splendor of the Lord and contemplate in his temple. (Psalm 27:4)

This is how we're meant to live—dwelling in the house of the Lord. David speaks of his desire to be in God's house continuously. Not only does he desire this, but he actively seeks it. If he thought of dwelling in God's house as only something to check off his list, he wouldn't use words like "desire" and "seek." I'm told that cod liver oil is good for you, but that's certainly not something I desire or seek after. David speaks from experience; he knows that dwelling in the Lord's house is pleasurable.

The word for "live" in Psalm 27:4 is *yashab* in Hebrew, which can also be used for "settle" or even "marry." This is no short stay in a motel; it's immersion in His house, preparing for our eternity by learning of Him and worshiping throughout our lives.

So where or what is God's house, and what is David writing about in the Psalms? The temple? The church? Heaven? The best answer is that God's house is wherever His glory is evident. Here on earth, we can experience His dwelling place when we, in faith and with a right spirit, seek to proclaim His glory in worship. Our church is a wonderful place to do this, where there's teaching from the Word about God's character, and fellowship in the body of Christ, and songs that help us worship God corporately with one voice.

But we should desire more from our walk with the Lord than just visiting His house once a week. We can settle our lives in the house of the Lord and experience the pleasure of constancy by dwelling in worship. As David says,

> *I maintain a pure lifestyle, so I can appear before your altar, O LORD, to give you thanks, and to tell about all your amazing deeds. O LORD, I love the temple where you live, the place where your splendor is revealed.* (Psalm 26:6-8)

The thrill of dwelling in the Lord's house is peace, joy, and intimacy with the Sovereign by whom we were created. However, we'll soon experience dwelling with God more tangibly for all eternity. In Revelation we get a foretaste of what His house and our final dwelling place is like:

> *Now I saw no temple in the city, because the Lord God — the All-Powerful — and the Lamb are its temple. The city does not need the sun or the moon to shine on it, because the glory of God lights it up, and its lamp is the Lamb.* (Revelation 21:22-23)

His house and city are full of His glory. We'll be inescapably enthralled by Him.

Here on earth, His glory, though present, is veiled by our sin and mortality. But we can still surround ourselves with His glory when we enter into His courts with praise and worship of His character. This is what dwelling in His house looks like here on earth — worshiping Him in a lifestyle of submission, love, and obedience that leads to an overflow of words and prayers of praise.

Dwelling in His house isn't asking for things constantly, which is a great way to make our prayer lives dry up. We don't experience the fullness of His glory when we're constantly asking for things, unless we're also bowing down before His love and omnipotence in providing for our needs. A needy or faithless child of God is no adornment to God's house filled with His glory.

So build your life of worship. Establish the rudiments of true worship—obedience, holiness, and a heart that's warm toward the Lord. Then build your palette with the vivid colors of the knowledge of God's attributes and doctrine. Adorn your spiritual life with an abundance of prayers and declarations of the majesty of the Most High. Pray and declare that our worship will grow deeper and stronger. That we'll dwell in His house constantly for all our days and take on His likeness. That the light of His glory declared from our lips will be more striking in the darkness of this world. That our crawl will become a walk, our walk a run, and our run a sprint to the finish line, where we'll enter into an eternity of worship in God's very presence.

Postlude

Praise the LORD!

Praise God in his sanctuary!

Praise him in the sky, which testifies to his strength!

Praise him for his mighty acts!

Praise him for his surpassing greatness!

Praise him with the blast of the horn!

Praise him with the lyre and the harp!

Praise him with the tambourine and with dancing!

Praise him with stringed instruments and the flute!

Praise him with loud cymbals!

Praise him with clanging cymbals!

Let everything that has breath praise the LORD!

Praise the LORD!

(Psalm 150)

Acknowledgments

Special thanks to:

Pastors Steve Hager,

Craig Landrum,

Allan Harris,

Jim Davis, and

Chris Mcknight

Notes

In chapter 1, D. A. Carson's quote is from *Worship by the Book*, edited by D. A. Carson (Grand Rapids: Zondervan, 2002).

In chapter 2, the J. I. Packer quote is from *Revelations of the Cross* (reprint ed.; Peabody, Massachusetts: Hendrickson Publishers, 2013).

In chapter 2, the N. T. Wright quote is from *Simply Christian: Why Christianity Makes Sense* (San Francisco: Harper One, 2016).

In Chapter 2, the John Piper quote is from the sermon "Worship: The Feast of Christian Hedonism," September 25, 1983; www.desiringGod.org.

In chapter 2, Lee Massey's comments on George Washington are from E. C. M'guire, *The Religious Opinions and Character of Washington*, reproduction edition (London: FB&c Ltd., 2015), 141-142. (Original ed: New York, Harper & Brothers, 1836.)

In chapter 2, the A.W. Tozer quote is from *Whatever Happened to Worship? A Call to True Worship*, A. W. Tozer, editor; compiled by Gerald B. Smith (Chicago: Moody, 2012).

In chapter 3, the Russell Moore quote is from *Tempted and Tried* (Wheaton, Illinois: Crossway, 2011).

In chapter 3, the New Year's prayer by Samuel Johnson is from *Prayers and Meditations*. (Third ed: London: H. R. Allenson, Ltd., 1785).

In chapter 4, the John Owen quote is from *The Works of John Owen, D. D.*, edited by Thomas Russell, M. A., vol. XIX (London: Paternoster Row, 1826).

In chapter 5, the Joni Eareckson Tada quote is from an interview 9/2017. Mrs. Tada is the founder/CEO of Joni and Friends.

In chapter 5, lyrics to "Turn Your Eyes upon Jesus" are by Helen H. Lemmel.

In chapter 6, the story of treasure hunter Mel Fisher is from the "Mel Fisher's Treasures" website, accessed at http://www.melfisher.com/SalvageOperations/TributeToMel .asp.

In chapter 6, the quote by Jonathan Edwards is from *The Works of Jonathan Edwards, Vol. 17: Sermons and Discourses, 1730-1733*, edited by Mark Valeri (New Haven, Connecticut: Yale University Press, 1999).

In chapter 7, the quote by A. W. Tozer is from *Born after Midnight* (Camp Hill, Pennsylvania: Christian Publications, Inc., 1959).

In chapter 10, the Charles Spurgeon quotation is from his *Morning and Evening* devotional, revised and updated ESV edition (Wheaton, Illinois: Crossway, 2003).

In chapter 10, the quote from David Guzik is from his "Enduring Word" commentary and can be accessed at https://enduringword.com/bible-commentary/romans-2.

In chapter 10, the Messala quote is from the motion picture *Ben-Hur*, directed by William Wyler, produced by Metro-Goldwyn-Mayer, 1959.

In chapter 11, the quoted hymn "O Lord, My Rock and My Redeemer" by Nathan Stiff is from Sovereign Grace Music.

In chapter 11, the Charles Spurgeon quotation is from *Spurgeon's Sermons Volume 19: 1873*, edited by Anthony Uyl (Woodstock, Ontario: Devoted Publishing, 2017).

In chapter 12, the A. W. Tozer quotation is from *The*

Knowledge of the Holy: The Attributes of God, Their Meaning in the Christian Life (New York: Harper, 1961).

In chapter 12, the Russell Moore quotation is from his website, accessed at https://www.russellmoore.com/2012/02/13/lets-have-more-worship-wars/.

In chapter 12, information contributing to the story of Charles Wesley was obtained from Christianity.com, accessed at https://www.christianity.com/church/church-history/timeline/1701-1800/charles-wesley-11630230.html.

In chapter 14, the quote from John Piper is from *Desiring God: Meditations of a Christian Hedonist* (Colorado Springs, Colorado: Multnomah, 1996).

Made in the USA
Coppell, TX
27 November 2023

24877533R00144